RUFFORD:
Its Past & Its Pec

by
Joan Rimmer

Landy Publishing
2006

ISBN 1 872895 71 9

A catalogue record of this book is available from the British Library.

Layout by A D Forth
Printed by the Nayler Group, Accrington Tel 01254 234247

Landy Publishing have also published:-

Lancashire's Medieval Monasteries by Brian Marshall
Traipsing from Lancashire Toll Bar: Bretherton,Croston,Hesketh Bank,Hoole,Tarleton, & Walmer Bridge in Focus by Betty Gilkes & Stan Pickles
Penwortham,Hutton & Longton in Focus by Catherine Rees
Preston in Focus by Stephen Sartin
Edgworth To Crowthorn; the Story of a Lancashire Children's Home by Anita D Forth
Play Up,Higher Walton: Football in a Lancashire Village 1882-2005 by Peter Holme
Life on the Lancaster Canal by Janet Rigby

A full list is available from Landy Publishing
"Acorns"
3 Staining Rise
Staining
Blackpool
FY3 0BU
Tel/Fax 01253 895678

CONTENTS

INTRODUCTION

The village of Rufford is situated on an area of higher ground between Martin Mere and the River Douglas and, many years ago, it was often isolated by floods until the *'sluice'* (channel) was cut to drain this part of the mere. The name is derived from the *'rough ford'* where the road from Mawdesley crossed the River Douglas or where the road to Burscough crossed the sluice. Another theory of the origin of the name Rufford is that it was named after the *'Ruff'* bird, the male of species having a frilly ruff round its neck in summer. The spelling of the village name has changed over the years. In 1212 it was *Ruchford*, in 1318 it was *Roughford*, in 1327 it was *Rughford* and in 1411 it was Roghford. Another spelling was *Rufforthe*.

At the time of the Domesday Book (1086,) Rufford, in the baronetcy of Penwortham, covered an area of one *'carucate'*. This was the amount of land that could be ploughed in one year and a day.

When the Manor of Rufford was owned by the Hesketh family of Rufford Old Hall, the estate extended to 2962 statute acres and covered the whole of Rufford with the exception of an estate belonging to the church.

The old village was centred in the area of Flash Lane, previously called *'The Flash'* (stretch of water). The area, known as *'The Great Croft'* could not develop because of the natural boundaries. The higher ground around the *Hesketh Arms Inn* was outside the main village and was known as *'The Moor'*. This appears to be confirmed by the fact that the land opposite the inn was shown on Henry Porter's 1763 map of the Township of Rufford, as the *'Cunnery,* which comes from *'conniniere,'* an old French word for rabbit warren. *'Coney'* (or *cony)* is an old word for rabbit.

Rufford was described by Peter Fleetwood Hesketh in his monumental book, *'Murray's Lancashire Architectural Guide'*, as

4

'a whitewashed village of Jacobean and Georgian cottages backed by the trees of the park'.

In later years, the wet ground was drained, the layout of the village changed, the population grew and the canal and railways were constructed. This resulted in the creation of new jobs and with increased mechanisation many of the old village occupations and trades disappeared.

Throughout these times, the Hesketh family and Martin Mere played an integral part in the history of the village and in the lives of its people.

....

This book came about through my father talking about his home village. This encouraged me to gather and record local information and to share this with past and present residents of Rufford.

Amongst those who have been helpful and generous with their time or loan of photographs are, Trevor Bridge, June Craven, Alice Dalton, Derek and Madge Dalton, Margaret Fairclough, John Forshaw, Heather Goodyear. Mrs Gottard, Sandra Gregory, Joe Grisedale, Maureen and David Huyton, Tom Latto, Rosemary and the late Fred Lee, Ken Lingard, Lily McLeod, Sandra McShane, Bill and Rhona Meadley, Judy Molyneux, Sarah Jane Morey, Beth and James Moss, Mrs Nanson, Mrs Parker, Brian and Winifred Porter, Gerry and Jean Rawsthorne, Margery Reynolds, Marion Sumner, Angela Turnbull, Paul Mullins (Rufford Old Hall), the manager at Mere Sands Wood, members of the Dover Fellowship Cycling Club and the staff at Tarleton and Skelmersdale libraries, Lancashire Record Office, Lancashire Site and Monuments and Lancashire Sound Archive, Clitheroe. My thanks also to those not listed here who have helped in any way and have given snippets of information, also to my family and friends for their continued encouragement. Special thanks to Stanley Lingard and the late Bertha Crocker, who spent many hours talking to me and sharing their memories of Rufford.

MARTIN MERE

"The Mere" has existed since the retreat of the ice at the end of the Pleistocene period (10,000 BC). When the ice melted, it left a clay-lined hollow and the Lancashire plain was created. The Domesday Book (1086) refers to *'Merretun'* meaning a settlement by the lake, and was the first historical reference to the mere.

Antiquarians say that the shoreline was covered in oak, birch, pine, ash and elder trees and that wild boar, wolves and deer roamed the forest. To the north of this forest, a tribe of Brythonic Celts had some strongholds around the banks of the River Douglas. The Romans also knew the Mere when they passed along the banks of the Douglas on their way from Wigan to Ribchester.

In earlier times the large expanse of water that extended from the River Douglas to Crossens and known as *'Linius'* or lake, was described by an old time writer as *'the greatest Meare in Lancastershire, 3 myles in length and 2 in breadth'*. An arm of the mere extended from Rufford to Scarisbrick and the ferry between the two villages was at one time manned by a Rufford man.

For many years the monks of Burscough Priory held the fishing rights on the mere and the remains of coracles and canoes discovered much later showed the repair marks of the monks. The catch was sold at the weekly Friday market in Rufford. The fish stall was on the site of the present police house where the fish stones were discovered when the road was widened in 1962. One monk would sell the fish while another preached from the market cross situated on the village green. These fishing rights had been disputed since the reign of King Edward III and in 1557, when Sir Thomas Hesketh held the rights, Henry Banastre and John Hunter, who disputed them, took action for *'assault and battery'* against him and some of his servants. Sir Thomas won the case.

6

Harold Broderick, in his 1902 book *'Martin* Mere' published by The Southport Society of Natural Sciences, described the boundaries of the mere as starting at the sluice near to Birch Hall, Tootle Lane, running north towards Holmeswood then on towards Banks, Scarisbrick, New Lane and Tarlscough to Clay Brow. The coast then went between Helm House and Tootle House and then back to the sluice near Birch Hall. According to local folk lore, the part of the Mere near to Rufford was reputed to have had a *'swallow hole'* where objects sank down and then re-appeared some distance away, and also a bottomless *'hell hole'*. The Mere stayed in its natural state until 1692 when work began on draining it to provide fertile agricultural land.

The legend - Martin Mere is connected with the legend of Sir Lancelot, son of Ban, the king of Beoit in Brittany, and his wife Queen Helen. A nymph, Vivian, took the infant Lancelot and jumped into the lake with him. There, according to the legend, he was educated in one of the subterranean caverns, hence his name, Lancelot du Lac. The name Lancelot was said by some to be the derivation of Lancashire or *'Lancelot-shire.'*
Lancelot was 18 years old when he joined the court of King Arthur, who, according to ancient chronicles, fought against the Saxons in four battles on the banks of the River Douglas. In January 1867, the son of Robert Ashcroft of Brick Kiln Farm ploughed up a tree trunk that was later identified as an ancient canoe or boat, thus proving that early Britons had crossed this stretch of water. Weapons and animal bones have been discovered alongside the Douglas and on the bed of the Mere.

Drainage of the Mere - In 1692, Thomas Hesketh of Bank Hall, Tarleton obtained an Act of Parliament to drain the mere in order to increase the acreage of arable land. In 1693, two thousand men were employed in the task but severe storms destroyed the sluices, the embankment and the flood gates and the mere was flooded. A second drainage attempt was made in 1717 but in 1750, the flood gates and embankment were again washed away. Although Mr Eccleston of Scarisbrick Hall drained part of the mere near to his estate and ploughed and harvested 200 acres of oats and barley, the area was flooded again in 1789. It was not until 1849 that Sir Thomas Dalrymple Hesketh implemented an efficient drainage system on the mere.

The Holmeswood pumping station in Wiggins Lane, built in 1849, was originally operated by wind power. In the 1920's the engines were gas-driven using anthracite. Mr Pickervance of Rufford transported this by horse and cart from New Lane station. In 1953 the engines were converted to diesel power and in the 1980s to electricity. The monitoring of the water levels and the control of the pumps are now the responsibility of the Environment Agency.

The pumping station at Wiggins Lane Holmeswood
used to drain the Mere

THE MANOR AND HALLS OF RUFFORD

After his victory at the battle of Hastings in 1066, William the Conqueror divided England into regions and the area that included Rufford was granted to Roger de Busle(Bussel), a Norman baron. He then left it to his son Richard. Between 1150 and 1160, Roger de Busle gave one *'plough land'* (the amount of land that could be ploughed by one team of 8 oxen in one year) in Rufford to the abbot at St Werburg's Abbey, Chester, who still held the land in 1212. It was through Richard that the Manor of Rufford became the property of the Fitton family who were connected to the Bussels by marriage. Maude Fytton (daughter and heiress of Richard Fytton) owned half of the manor of Rufford and she married William de Heskayth in 1276. He was described as *'a landless man of unknown parentage.'* According to Baines' *'History of Lancashire'*, this Sir William Heskayth was the great-great-great grandson of Hellarth, the first known member of the Hesketh family The name *'Hesketh '* is derived from the Norse word for a horse racing course.

The other half of the manor was owned by Edmund Fytton whose daughter Alice married William's grandson, Sir John Heskayte. The Hesketh family then held the manor as an unbroken estate until it was sold in 1906.

Rufford Old Hall

Although the origins of the Hesketh family are unsure, it is thought that they originated from Hesketh with Becconsall, a village a few miles north of Rufford. It was Sir William Heskayte, *'Lord of Heskayte and Becconsawe'*, living in 1276, who married Maude Fytton, co- heiress to the Manor of Rufford. A descendent, Sir Thomas Hesketh, who held the manor between 1412 and 1458, built or replaced an earlier hall on the site. The Great Hall is all that remains of a house built by Sir Robert Hesketh in 1530. A brick wing was added in 1662 and

9

the service wing was rebuilt about 1725 and refurbished in 1820.

Two places in the vicinity have been suggested as earlier homes of the Heskeths and Fyttons. One was a hunting lodge on the site of Holmeswood Hall to the west and, approximately one mile to the north of the Old Hall, the site of an ancient house and moat is shown on an old map of the area. The Rev Bulpit (rector of Banks) suggested in his *Notes of Southport and District 1908*, that the site, known as *'Peels Platt'* (a *'peel'* was a house with a tower for defence and a *'platt'* was a flat bridge over a water course) was perhaps the old home of the Fytton family.

The Island, Peel's Platt surrounded by a moat is thought to have been the home of the Fitton family whose daughter Maud married into the Hesketh family.

When the family moved to the New Hall, the Old Hall was tenanted by various employees including the Lowe family but the banqueting hall was still used as the village school. In 1820 the hall was altered and refurbished and in 1826 it was occupied by Thomas Henry Hesketh (1799-1842) and his wife Annette Bomford. It then became the home of the Dowager Lady Hesketh until her death in 1879. Other tenants of the hall included Thomas Ogilvy, George Holmes, James King and Robert Rankin.

Sir Thomas Fermor Hesketh, the eighth baron, made the Old Hall his home until the family moved to live at Easton Neston, Northamptonshire. In 1936 he presented the hall, endowments and eleven acres of garden and land, to the National Trust.

The Ghosts of Rufford Old Hall

There are several versions of the *'Grey Lady'* story but no evidence or dates for the people or events mentioned. The most popular story concerns Ann Elizabeth Hesketh whose husband was called to fight in one of the Scottish wars soon after their wedding. Some time later a soldier was passing through the village on his way home from the war and told her that her husband was making his way back. She waited in vain, refused to eat, took to her bed and then died. It is said that on her death bed she promised her spirit would stay at the hall to await her love's return. The story told is that her ghost, solid in form but casting no shadow, has often been seen walking up and down *'Beech Walk'* between the Old Hall and the parish church and on one occasion it is said that she enjoyed listening to the piano in a ground floor apartment.

Another version of the same story is that Elizabeth was waiting for her betrothed to return and complete the wedding preparations but later heard that he was dead. Her broken hearted spirit is said to haunt the upper passageways in the hall.

Two other ghost stories connected to the Old Hall are that the ghostly figure of a man dressed in Elizabethan costume has been seen by the fireplace in the Great Hall and Queen Elizabeth 1 is said to have appeared in the Dining Room but vanished when anyone approached her.

William Shakespeare

In about 1580, Stratford teacher, John Cottom, a tenant of Alexander Hoghton of Preston, sent his 17 years old pupil William Shakespeare to be an assistant teacher at Alexander's home. When William's acting talent was recognised it seemed reasonable to transfer him to the Rufford home of Sir Thomas Hesketh who was a relative of Hoghton's wife Elizabeth. Sir Thomas (1526-1588), a known patron of actors and musicians who had his own company of players, was introduced to William Shakeshafte (the Lancashire variant for Shakespeare) in 1581. He only stayed for a few months before returning to Stratford in the summer of 1582. His stay in Rufford is upheld by scholars who have produced evidence to support the facts.

Rufford New Hall

The 1735 plan (now in the Lancashire Record Office) of the proposed Neo-classical mansion which would become known as the *New Hall* was commissioned by Thomas Hesketh (1698-1735). In 1748, his son, also Thomas (1727-1778), married Harriet Cowper and by 1760 he had built the New Hall. The next occupants were his cousin Sir Robert Hesketh (1728-1796) and his wife, the former Jacintha Dalrymple. Their son Sir Thomas Dalrymple Hesketh (1777-1842) greatly extended the property in 1798 when he married Sophie Hinde. A large and impressive extension, designed by John Foster, surveyor to Liverpool Corporation, was built.

The grounds included a Dutch garden, a rose garden, a lily pond, a gardener's cottage *(Springwood Lodge)*, a stable block and a lake with an island. Winter ice from the lake was stored in the nearby Ice House. This was built at the same time as the hall and was constructed of sandstone, brick and earth. It was a subterranean ice chamber that was approached by a brick, vaulted passage on the North West side, covered with a mound of earth and surrounded by a circular *'Ha-Ha'* (a sunken fence bordering a park or garden). The stored ice was said to have lasted until well into the summer.

Entrance chamber to the ice house in the park. It was covered with a mound of earth and surrounded by a circular 'Ha Ha'.

The New Hall and park were put up for auction in the estate sale of 1906 but were unsold. In 1912, the property was purchased by Lancashire County Council for £21, 656. It was converted into

13

a pulmonary hospital, then into a convalescent hospital before it closed in 1987. The site was sold and in 1991, a planning application was submitted to West Lancashire District Council for the building of a hotel, golf course and country club. An archaeological evaluation was undertaken by Lancaster University Archaeological Unit and the plans did not reach fruition. The site was resold, planning applications were submitted to the district council in 1996 and 1997 to convert the stable block into mews houses, to refurbish and extend the hall and to build houses in the Springwood area of the park. The first houses were built in 1998.

New Road before the bungalows were built, with 'Rufford Lodge' and the New Hall gates.

The rose garden and New Hall when it was a pulmonary hospital. The beds were on the open veranda as fresh air was thought to be therapeutic for tuberculosis patients.

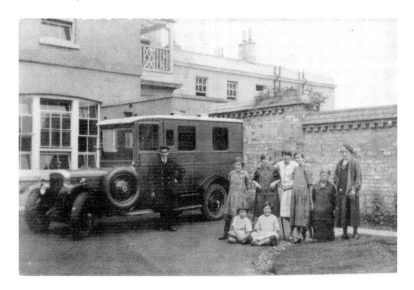

Convalescent patients outside the rear of the new hall when it was used as a pulmonary hospital. Were they going on an outing in the ambulance?

MARKET DAY AND THE OLD VILLAGE

On November 2nd 1339, King Edward III granted a charter to Sir William de Heskayte, entitling him to hold a weekly Friday market and an annual fair on May 1st, the feast day of the apostles St Philip and St James. By the 16th century, the original grant was lost and on 3rd November 1573, Sir Thomas Hesketh obtained a Deed of Confirmation of Edward's Charter from Queen Elizabeth I.

One reason that was given for holding fairs on feast days was that people connected things that happened in their every day life with the duty that they owed to God, '*the Giver of good things*'. The arrangement of markets varied according to their size and importance. The smallest, usually held in villages like Rufford, would be under the sole control of the lords or their bailiffs.

The Rufford fair and market were held on the village green that was situated along the Preston- Liverpool Road at the junction with Church Road. (This road was shown on various censuses as *Chapel Lane* (1851), *Church Street* (1881), *Church Lane* (1891) and *Chapel Lane* again in 1901. The market cross and village stocks were on the site but the stocks were later lost and the cross was removed in 1818.

In the church magazine of May 1910, Rev Proctor, a historian and rector of Rufford, wrote that he had read in an old chronicle that the fair day was the maddest and merriest of days. Stalls were placed around the green and a large variety of goods were offered for sale. A Margery Kilsha had baskets of pullet eggs, spring chickens, young ducks, fresh eggs, vegetables and bunches of flowers. Cuthbert Mayson, nick-named '*Oat bread Mayson*', sold '*loaves, riddle cakes, thar cakes, throdden bread, treacle bunnocks, sweet meats and sugar plums.*' Dick Forshaw and his wife Nancy sold '*pea soup, black puddings, fried fish, nettle beer and spiced ale.*'

Although the usual fair activities took place on the village green, there were also more blood thirsty sporting activities such as bull baiting and cock fighting. These took place on a plot of land (behind the present *Beech House*) called the *'Cock pit.'*

In later years the weekly market ceased and in 1846 the annual fair became the *'Rufford Agricultural Show'*.

The old village

The majority of the cottages in the village or township of Rufford where the agricultural workers lived were originally situated north of the *'Great Croft'* along Flash Lane, Park Lane, (which was a westward extension of Flash Lane,) and Mere Sands. When the New Hall was extended and Lord Hesketh enclosed the park, many of the workers' cottages were demolished in 1818. In a letter to his agent William Shakeshaft, Lord Hesketh showed an uncompromising attitude to his tenants whom he blamed for the condition of the properties. He said that the cottages should be pulled down without exception as he was determined to get rid of the nuisance. The villagers were relocated to other properties within the village, many moving to the northern end of the village which was referred to as *'North Fields'*. A map of part of the township made by Henry Porter in 1763, showed Flash Lane extending westwards towards Holmeswood but with the creation of the park, the road was diverted to the south of the New Hall.

When George Fermor Hesketh (1849-1924) inherited the estate, he built some good semi-detached cottages with large gardens, as previously very little had been done to improve the living conditions of the estate workers. Although now extended and improved, many of these cottages, including *'Cross House'* and *'Wayside Cottage'* in Brick Kiln Lane and some in Mill Hey (*'hey'* means field), can still be seen today.

17

DEMOGRAPHY: HATCHINGS, MATCHINGS & DESPATCHINGS

At the time of the Domesday Book (1086,) the population of Lancashire was less than 2000 and they lived along the coastal plain within 20 miles of the Irish Sea.

An Act of Parliament in 1793 separated the township of Rufford from the parish of Croston where the births, marriages and deaths of Rufford people were recorded in the register of that parish church.

Some of the earliest recorded baptisms of Rufford people were for the year 1632 and included Elizabeth Cooton on April 15th, Margaret Watkinson on May 13 and Susan Ashbourne on June 5th.

The marriage on June 28th 1632 of Rufford villagers Roger Gooden and Ellin Wright, and of Richard Light and Elizabeth Caumer on October 22nd 1670 were also recorded in the Croston register. The church registers for Rufford date from 1670 and record the marriage of Richard Alty and Ann, daughter of Richard Tootel on November 17th 1672. (The registers for Rufford, 1632-1812, are published in a book by the Lancashire Parish Register Society - Vol 115).

7 burials of Rufford residents at Rufford Chapel were recorded in the Croston register in 1540, 1638, 1639, 1650, 1653, 1657 and 1658.

Some figures taken at random:-

	1670	1671	1700	1701	1831	1832
Baptisms	10	13	31	14	104	82
Marriages	1	0	1	1	2	5
Burials	19	16	12	11	50	56

In order to support the country's growing woollen trade, an Act of Congress of 1678 decreed that everyone was to be buried in woollen shrouds.

Due to the flooding of the surrounding, low-lying ground, Rufford was often isolated and roads were impassable. With lack of transport and low wages, villagers did not travel far and did not appear to marry people who lived outside the village. In the old church yard the same surnames have been recorded on the gravestones for many generations from 1632 to 1930. A few examples are:-

Alty-No of graves	19	containing 47	Average life span 61 years
Ashcroft	24	76	51 years
Baldwin	13	22	68 years
Banks/Bank/			
Bavnk	10	13	59 years
Barron	13	34	60 years
Bridge	16	46	65 years
Caunce	48	114	58 years
Hesketh	11	26	58 years
Lea	10	25	63 years

From 1930, when the new church yard was made, until the present day, some of the old family names remain but new surnames reflex the changing population.

Ashcroft –			
No of graves 14	containing 20	Average life span	74.6 years
Caunce	17	24	75.4 years
Sephton	13	20	75 years
Martland	6	6	65 years
Taylor	4	5	70.4 years
Bridge	4	7	70.5 years
Smith	3	3	69 years

During this period there was only one grave in each of the following old family names; Alty, Baldwin, Barron, and Lea.

During one period, the words *'stranger,' ' pauper'*, *'vagrant'* or *'traveller'* appeared on the records and the death of George, *'the son of a common beggar,'* was recorded on 7th August 1757. Between 1806 and December 1811 the cause of death was recorded in the parish register and in Rufford these included *'dropsy,' 'consumption', 'apoplexy,' 'measles,' 'asthma', 'smallpox','* *typhus fever'* and occasionally as the result of a burn. On 20th November 1808, John Caunce froze to death.

Due to being near the stagnant pools of the Mere, the *'ague'* (a malarial fever with shivering fits) was prevalent in the area but this improved when the Mere was drained. In his book of 1836, Baines recorded that the conditions had obviously improved at that time as the parish clerk was 91 years of age.

In his talk to the *Historical Society of Lancashire and Cheshire* on the 12th December 1907, the Rev W G Proctor said that between 1740 and 1810 the population was double the number it was in 1907. During the 18th century the population numbers remained fairly constant and in 1821, the population of 1073 was the greatest on record.   There were 162 inhabited houses with 189 families (153 were employed in agriculture), 17 males aged 70-80, two females aged 80-90 and one who was over 90 years old.

The number of households had dramatically increased since 1663 when the Hearth Tax returns for Lady Day showed that there were 42 properties in the village. Some obviously had more than one hearth as the number of actual hearths was 69 for the same year.

Population on Census Day

1811 – 998	1841 – 866	1871 – 819	1901 - 782
1821 – 1073	1851 – 861	1881 - 905	
1831 – 869	1861 – 865	1891 – 816	

RIVER, ROAD, CANAL AND RAILWAY

The River Douglas, first named *'Asland'* , which comes from the Norse word for *'ash tree'*, emptied into the Irish Sea at Crossens before sand dunes blocked the river's passage and forced the channel northwards to the estuary of the River Ribble at Hesketh Bank. In 1719 an Act of Parliament was passed to make the River Douglas navigable and despite opposition from the Hesketh family and other landowners the *'Douglas Navigation Company'* was formed. This company was in operation until 1783 when it was bought by the *'Leeds and Liverpool Canal Company'*.

In 1634 the old bridge over the river at Rufford, shown on maps as *'White's Bridge'*, decayed and the magistrate at Wigan requested William and Michael Mawdesley from Mawdesley and Robert Hesketh of Rufford to find skilled men to undertake repairs to the bridge. This was done at an estimated cost of £9.0.0!

The road from Holmeswood originally continued up Flash Lane to join the main road from Burscough to Preston (known as *'Preston Road'*) near to the present village hall. The roads were often deeply rutted and dangerous. Along Preston Road to the south of the village, a path or causeway (approximately 2 feet wide and paved with pebbles) was constructed at the side of the road for the use of people travelling on foot. White posts were erected between the causeway (a raised road over wet ground) and the road to prevent horses and carts from straying onto the path. In 1743 the road was greatly improved and, following the Turnpike Act 1771, the road through Rufford, part of the 30 miles from Liverpool to Preston, was turnpiked. Economic expansion had produced increased traffic and the tolls raised income to maintain them. The first stage coach passed through Rufford in 1751 and in later years, passengers would stay overnight at the *'Hesketh Arms Inn'* where there was stabling for 12 horses.

The Rufford branch of the Leeds and Liverpool Canal (known as the *'new cut'*) was completed in 1781 and joined the River Douglas at Sollom Lock. From there the canal followed the course of the river northwards to Tarleton. This provided an important connection from the main canal at Burscough to the estuary of the River Ribble and on to the Irish Sea. The Rufford lock is Grade 2 listed and is built of dressed sandstone blocks with wood and iron gates. The branch is also a biological heritage site because of the range of plant life found there.

Negotiations took place between the canal company and Sir Thomas Hesketh regarding the purchase of land for a towpath. The towpath along the canal in Rufford was built in the 1760s and on one occasion after horses replaced men in hauling the boats, Lord Hesketh complained that Richard Dobson of Sollom had allowed his horses to damage fences on his ground while towing boats.

The two canal wharfs in Rufford were busy places, loading and unloading cargoes of agricultural produce, stone, ballast and timber. Manure and *'night soil'* from Liverpool (where there was a special *'manure dock'*) were delivered to Fearns Farm further along the waterway and to most agricultural areas. In 1829 the charge for this service was one farthing per ton per mile. Signs of the Causeway wharf, at the side of the road leading to Burscough, can still be seen today.

The locks on the Rufford branch of the Leeds and Liverpool canal.They are Grade 2 listed and constructed of dressed sandstone blocks and iron gates.

The old boat house was on an inlet on the canal. This inlet was known as a *'whamming pool'* that was made to enable boats to turn around. The Hesketh family had their own boat house nearer to the Old Hall and a bridge over the canal. The stone bases of the bridge can still be seen on the banks of the canal. Horse drawn barges carrying coal from Wigan, would use the weighbridge opposite to the Fermor Arms Inn and the bargees, who slept on their boats, would stable the horses at the inn. Horses gave way to diesel engined boats in the 1930s and 1940s.

The old road bridge over the canal was replaced by a more sturdy construction about 1960.

When the Liverpool to Preston railway was first proposed in 1844 it was rejected but this decision was later reversed and finally received the Royal Assent on 18 August 1846. Rufford station was opened in 1848 by the *West Lancashire Railway Company* who operated the line until 1897 when it was taken over by the *Lancashire and Yorkshire Railway Company.* The site included a goods yard with large sidings where loads of produce, coal and timber were handled. (This was to the left of the present road). On one occasion a farmer had purchased some cows at a local market and transported them by train to Rufford station. He then had to walk them from Rufford to Hesketh Bank!

Various railway incidents were reported in the local papers of the time. The 'Preston Chronicle 'of 1 February 1851 reported on a tragic accident had occurred at Rufford station. When the porter, William Hesketh heard a groaning noise he went to investigate and found John Halton lying across the line. The given explanation was that he had been drinking in Ormskirk and had jumped from the train before it had reached the station. His injuries were so severe that he died 4 hours later in the station house. On 3 May of the same year it was reported that 300 teetotallers from Liverpool arrived at the station. Accompanied by fife and drum bands, they marched to the New Hall, listened to speeches and danced in the grounds before leaving the village on the 8.00pm train.

In 1870 two gentlemen who were visiting Rufford described the station as 'clean, sweet smelling and rural looking' and when, on the wall, they saw blue shields with sheaves of wheat in the centre, they asked the station master for an explanation. He was quite indignant when he realised that the gentlemen were unaware of the fact that the shields were the coat of arms of the lord of the manor, Lord Hesketh, who had his own waiting room on the station though nothing remains of this today.

The arrival of the railway was a boon to the village people who were able to travel more easily to the shops and markets in Ormskirk and Preston.

Taken from the canal bridge looking towards Sollom with the canal company building on canal wharf.

The whamming pool and the old boathouse. In the distance, the bases of the Hesketh private bridge can be seen on either side of the canal.

25

Loading bales of straw in the station goods yard with the station master looking on about 1910

From left to right: the station house, waiting rooms, wooden crossing gates and the signal box. One of the waiting rooms was for the exclusive use of the Hesketh family.

Looking down Station Road towards the level crossing. The weigh bridge, used as a coal yard by *'Rufford Produce Company'* is on the right.This building is now part of *'Fettlers Wharf Marina'.*

THE VILLAGE CONSTABLE, LAW AND ORDER

Although Hewitson, in *'Our Country Churches and Chapels'* (1872) described the village as *'exquisitely pastoral and had no vagrants or 'dark horses'*, Rufford people had been involved in *'incidents'* from as early as 1354 when two local men were charged with taking fish from *'Le Wyke'* in North Meols, (a small creek of Martin Mere). In court their plea was that as the Mere had common fishing rights and the Wyke was part of the Mere they had no case to answer. For several centuries there have been keepers of the peace in Rufford. Giles Baldwin, a 17th century High Constable was described as *'a merry man who cared little about events that happened in the village provided that he received his salary plus a bag of buns at Christmas and a basket of eggs at Easter'*. However, one fair day he was called to a fight between Evan Caunce, a blacksmith from Holmeswood and Jim Cauntin from Rufford and despite the fact that both men were described as *' being more dead than alive'*, the High Constable was unable to separate them.

During a sermon in 1818, the Rev R Pearson preached that the villages of Rufford and Holmeswood were *'notorious for lawlessness and sin'*. An unconfirme report said that a young Rufford man had been executed for poaching.

Because of his great strength, physique and suitability, the young Edward Bridge 1773-1865 *'The Hero of Rufford'* was asked to be a parish constable.

The Petty Constable in the 1820s was Richard Bridge who was paid an annual salary of £9.14s.2d though his duties were undefined.

Due to the presence of footpads, vagrants and thieves in the village, Daniel Baron was appointed in 1827 to patrol the village during the winter months. There was no mention of a wage but he was provided with a lantern (cost 3/6d) and a rattle which had cost two shillings.

In 1851 the police constable was Francis Fell and in 1861 it was Edward Holding. They were members of the ('*Rural Police*') Lancashire Constabulary whose patrol officers came onto the streets about 1840. The earlier ones had been appointed by the local magistrates. During this time, the majority of villagers kept a shotgun in their homes and accidents or incidents that occurred were often reported in the local papers.

An inquest was held at the '*Hesketh Arms Inn*' in January 1892 into the death at Holmeswood of an Ormskirk yeoman who had borrowed a double barrelled shotgun without the owner's permission, and had suffered a fatal injury while trying to shoot a hare.

Another shotgun incident in November 1900 resulted in the tragic suicide of Eliza Ashcroft, a servant at Gornall's Farm Holmeswood. Although there had been nothing to indicate her intent, she had left a goodbye letter to her aunt.

The '*Preston Chronicle*'(14th April 1900) reported that, on 8th November of the previous year, a Rufford Man, Thomas Sephton who was a member of the '*Anti- Vaccination Society*, was fined 20 shillings plus costs for failing to have his child vaccinated.

Over the years the police station has been housed in various properties in the village. The first one was situated in a thatched cottage next to '*Beech House*' on the turnpike road (now Liverpool Road). Ambrose Tart was the officer in 1881 and moved to lodge at '*The Apiary*', Holly Lane on his retirement. In 1897, Robert Baldwin was appointed the constable with a salary of £3 per year and he was followed in 1901 by Hartley Pickles. These were local men appointed in addition to the '*new police*'

The station then moved to a property next to the smithy. This had been the home of a Mr Pilkington, who, on retiring from work, built the detached house and later sold it to the Lancashire Police Authority, then called '*The Standing Joint Committee*' It was used in the 1920s when PC Turner was the

29

officer. In the 1940s and 1950s there were two village police men: PC Henry who lived at the police station and PC Griffin who lived across the road at *'Lawn Villas'*.

In the late 1950s the present police station was built across the road from the old one.

Rufford Parish Church & School Fund.

Grand Fete and Bazaar

IN

RUFFORD PARK
(By kind permission of SIR THOMAS FERMOR-HESKETH, Bart.)

Thursday, 2nd July, 1925,
GATES OPEN AT 3 O'CLOCK.

Opening 3-30, by LADY FERMOR-HESKETH.

Chairman ~ H. ALTY, Esq.

AND

Saturday, 4th July, 1925,
GATES OPEN AT 2 O'CLOCK.

Opening 2-30, by Mrs. HENRY TYRER, "Bewcastle," Lathom.

Chairman ~ LIEUT.-COL. SEDDON BROWN, J.P.

Admission to Park : Thursday 1/-, Saturday 6d. (Children under 15 years, half-price)

Accommodation for Motors and Bicycles on the Park.

" *You wish us well ; but still, ye ken, We need your gowd for a' that.*"

THEY PLOUGHED THE FIELDS AND SCATTERED THE GOOD SEED ON THE LAND – FARMS AND FARMING

In 1824, Rufford was a *'village, township and parish in the Hundred and Deanery of Leyland'*. ('*Hundred*' was an ancient area of administration deriving from the area having supplied one hundred armed knights to serve the king).

From the middle of the 12th century the community were agriculturalists whose whole life was centred around the plough. The area covered 2,962 statute acres and comprised 1,194 acres of ploughed land, 1,463 acres of meadow and pasture, 205 acres of wood and trees plus 97 acres of gardens. The soil was *'good vegetable loam, easily worked but with low fertility that* would *be improved with good farming methods, generous liming and fertilizing'*. The many marl pits throughout the village (now filled) showed that, during the 18th century, '*marl*' (calcareous clay) was dug up and used to improve the soil.

Flax was grown on the low lying ground around Rufford before the importation of Irish flax in the 16th century and locally grown reeds, which grew on wet land, were supplied to the Mawdesley basket makers. In the 1920s there were '*twig*' (reed) beds at the side of Causeway Lane before the row of houses were built.

Following the draining of Martin Mere, farms were established on the reclaimed land. By the middle of the 18th century the majority of local men were employed in agriculture and by 1871 women were also employed to help with planting potatoes and spreading manure.

Before the mechanisation of farming, large numbers of people were needed to work the land and accidents did occur. The '*Preston Chronicle*' of 26th July 1851 reported that Mr Baldwin was loading hay in a field belonging to Mr Hurst, a Rufford farmer, when the horse chain became entangled with the cart shaft and the horse, cart and Mr Baldwin were dragged into the canal. The same edition reported on the death of John Reynolds. He worked on another farm in the village and had playfully thrown some potatoes at Ann Caunce and Margaret Wright but when Ann pretended to strike John with a pitchfork, she slipped and the fork cut his leg. He died the following week. On 5th April 1851, in the same paper, it was reported that many acres of land had recently been drained and large crops of potatoes and beans had been sown or planted.

The '*Ormskirk Advertiser*' of 14th December 1858 reported that the farmers of Rufford had arranged to help the widow of Henry Porter by ploughing some ground. 14 ploughmen, 37 horses and drivers had ploughed a 4 acre field in 6 hours. Mrs Porter rewarded the men by providing an excellent supper and experienced farmers said it was the best ploughing that they had seen. Potatoes were the most important crop grown in the village. In November and December 1878, 1000 tons per month were transported from Rufford station and it was claimed that 50 loads of potatoes were sent daily to Ormskirk. The fact that William Skirving from Liverpool sold Robert Alty 30lbs of best red clover seed in 1836 confirms that hay was also a crop grown locally. When covering the Rufford Agricultural Show in later years, the same newspaper reported that farmers were encouraged to apply manure to increase yields per acre and to reduce waste with the hope of increasing prosperity. Mr Harcourt Clare of Lancashire County Council, who had opened the May 1908 show, said that Rufford farmers were '*practical men and the best farmers in the countryside'*.

FARMS IN RUFFORD

(Acres, roods and perches are mentioned in this section and for clarification one perch equated to 30 1/4 square yards and one rood to ¼ of an acre).
The original settlers on the Hesketh estate held their farms under leases for '*three lives*' which were often those of the farmer, his wife and eldest son.
Until the early 20th century there were 20 working farms in Rufford plus small farms attached to the '*Fermor Arms Inn* 'and the '*Hesketh Arms Inn*'. The farms were owned by the Hesketh Estate and were mostly tenanted. Although they were arable farms they all had stables for the working horses and kept cows, pigs and hens to provide the family with milk, meat and eggs. The tithe schedule of 1839 identified that many of the cottages in the village also had a shippon, pig cote, orchard and garden. (Tithe was a tax of one tenth or a tenth part of the annual produce of land or labour and was paid to support the clergy and church.)

Fearns Farm, Preston Road
'*Fearns Farm*' had been in one branch of the Ashcroft family for many years. These Ashcrofts and the Ashcrofts of '*Church Farm*', '*Brick Kiln Farm*' and '*Folly Farm*' were all descendents of a Phillip Ascroft who died in 1690. (Spelling variations frequently occur).

Fearns Farm Liverpool Road, formerly known as '*Ferns Farm*' because of the number of these plants that grew in the grounds.
The '*Paddy House*', now extended, adjoins the house on the right.

33

The first farm house, a single storey, thatched cottage with very thick walls was called 'The Ferns' because of the large numbers of these plants that were growing around the cottage. There were two turf ovens in the house. Turf was cut from the fields, dried in the ovens and then stacked outside near the back door. There was also an L-shaped pantry with cheese shelves. The second house was joined to the shippons and was built of brick. The present house, built in 1808, has some of the original stones from the first house built into the walls and contains attics and cellars and a number of steps leading up to the back door. These were needed because the surrounding, low lying ground, known as 'Fearns Moss', was susceptible to flooding. A 'shant' for the Irish workmen adjoined the main house at one side. The original arable farm changed to a dairy farm in 1910 when one of the Ashcroft family married a farmer's daughter from Longridge. She made cheese and delivered this and milk around the village in a pony and trap.

Robert Ashcroft was the farmer in 1741 and various members of the same family continued to tenant the farm for many years. The 98 acres, 0 roods and 28 perches farm included shippons for 12 cows, stables, piggeries, hen sheds, a large orchard and a pond. A parcel of ground near to the canal and the station called 'Holland Meadow' was rented from the church and farmed by the family in 1906. The farm was sold for £4,400 in 1906 to the tenant, Charles Ashcroft. He was followed by his son Philip. Charles' daughter Margery recently found some black material wrapped round pipe work in the attic that has been identified as skirts and waistcoats belonging to her great-grandmother, who died in 1843.

Moss Side Farm, Sandy Lane
Although the present farm, built in the early 1850s, is situated on the edge of the nearby wood, a map of 1845 and old foundations shows that the original buildings were sited

among the trees in a more easterly direction. A rent of £202 was paid by George Caunce in 1872 for the 110 acre farm. Some early 20th century tenants were James Dalton, Richard Baron and Jack Rhodes. In 1906, William Dobson, the tenant of the 113 acre farm, paid a tithe rent of £ 17.9.9d and a land tax of £1.3.8d. The farm was not sold at the 1906 estate auction but was sold privately in 1932.

Field House Farm, Preston Road

Although the date of the original farm is not known, John Bridge was the tenant in 1842. The farm had a shippon for three cows, a brick building containing a two-stall stable with loft, a loose box, a two-division pig cote and twenty acres of land, The farm house was a well built brick and stone dwelling and was reputed to have had a ghost. The villagers knew the farm as *'the boggart house'* because in the early 20th century when Mr T C Porter was the tenant, a clean towel had been left out one night and in the morning it was covered with dirty hand marks. In 1872 the tenant, John Bridge, paid a rent of £42.12.0d.

Note the spelling of the Field House Farm, Liverpool Road, which was known to the villagers as the *'Boggart House'* because of *'strange happenings'* seen by a past tenant.

Home Farm- later known as 'Park Farm'

Situated at the end of Lovers Lane, the farm was built on the highest piece of ground in the village and it is thought that there had been previous buildings on the site for many years. The farmhouse and buildings were built as the *'home farm'* to the New Hall when it was built in 1798. The large walled garden was used to provide fresh fruit and vegetables for the family at the hall.

Details from a book containing directions from Lord Hesketh to his steward William Shakeshaft in 1809 showed that livestock (horses, pigs, sheep and asses) had to be disposed of when they were unprofitable and some labourers were to be laid off. Also, land that had been destroyed by sheep was to be sown with barley, white clover and hay and Shakeshaft was to take guidance from local farmers, particularly Richard Mayor.

Some of the farm bailiffs mentioned in the censuses were – George Storey, 1851; Thomas Kelsall, 1881; and Thomas Howarth, 1901.

In the early 20th century Mark Hunter lived there and in 1945, Jack Greenwood, his wife Nell and family lived there when Mr Demain was the manager.

In 1906 the rent for the 157 acres, 3 roods and 7 perches farm was £226 and in 1936 it was purchased by Walter Southworth. Some of the farm buildings were demolished and in 2002 the remaining buildings were converted into private dwellings.

Flash Farm, Flash Lane

Flash farm was built by Daniel Alty and his wife, the former Mary Dandy and he lived there until his death in 1853. The farm was situated on the left of the lane and to the side and rear of Hermitage Farm. In 1872 Susan Caunce paid an annual rent of £115 for the 46 acres. In 1891 it was tenanted by James Caunce, in 1906 by William Yates (who paid a rent of £107.1.11 for the 54 acres) and in 1910 by John Caunce.

Hermitage Farm, Flash Lane

Edward Bridge, a former bailiff to the Hesketh estate, built *'Hermitage Farm'* on land given to him by Thomas Hesketh. The farm dates from approximately 1675, the same time that *'Grey Gutter Farm'* (the home of the Bridge family for many years) was built. . The farm house was to the left of Flash Lane and the farm buildings were on the opposite side of the lane. Two large pieces of family furniture were found there, a large cupboard in a wall with the inscription *'Jane Bridge 1678'* and a press with the inscription *'Edward Bridge and Jane Bridge 1691'*. The coat of arms of the Bridge family was on an outside wall. Because inscriptions were rare on farm house walls and because the tomb of Edward Bridge (died on 1 January 1717) was originally inside the church, it was thought that he was of *'gentle stock'* (good breeding). The name of the farm is said to be connected with the fact that chantry priests had once lived there. (See later for more on this).

'The Hermitage', Flash Lane was built using the materials from the old farmhouse after it was demolished. The thatched roof was destroyed by fire and replaced with slates.

Looking up Flash Lane with Hermitage Farm on the left and the farmyard on the right. *'Daisy Cottage'* is in the centre of the picture

Church House Farm, Church Road

This was the original home farm for Rufford Old Hall. Before the building of Diamond Jubilee Road in 1897 to celebrate the sixtieth anniversary of Queen Victoria's accession to the throne, the farm gardens adjoined the church yard, thus, no stone wall was needed to the south side of the church. Some of the tenants were Robert Alty (1825,) Ellen Barron (1839,) Edward Bridge (1851,) Robert Baldwin between 1881 and 1891 and Robert Ashcroft in 1906. In November 1906, Thomas Porter purchased the 15- acre farm for £3000. A modern wall plaque on the wall of the new house suggests that there was a building on the site in 1667 when the present *Manor Farm* house was two farm workers' cottages. They were made into one dwelling and the two bricked-up front doors are still visible today. The farm which had also been known as *'Manor Farm'* and *'Manor House Farm'* was occupied by Mr Hadfield during the second World War and then it was purchased by the Bates family Today the rebuilt farm house is a private dwelling and the land is used as a marina for canal boats.

Lane End Farm, Liverpool Road

For many years this was the home of the Bridge family and in 1906 the tenant was Henry Yates. He paid a rent of £185.10s and a tithe rent of 12s.6d for the 90 acres, 1 rood and 26 perches. (Further information about the farm is in the section on Methodism.) The late Bertha Crocker nee Yates, a descendent of the Yates of Grey Gutter Farm, and her family, were the last occupants of this farm which is now a private dwelling.

Grey Gutter Farm, Liverpool Road

The farm was situated on Liverpool Road near to the site of the early village green and the farm house was built for Henry and Mary Banks in 1675. According to Rev Bulpit the property contained some interesting furniture including an oak bedstead engraved with the initials 'HB' and 'MB (Henry and Mary Banks). The initials were also on a date stone set into the outside wall the building had a platform where priests hid during the Reformation and a small cupboard in the fireplace wall where tea was kept hidden as it was an expensive and scarce commodity. When Mr Yates, the tenant, climbed up the stone 'garner' (store or granary) steps on the outside of the building, he was able to get into a V shaped opening at the top of the wall and walk round the inside chimney stack. The farm stayed in the Yates family until it was demolished in 1962 to make way for the new length of road.

In 1872 Richard Yates paid a rent of £ 87 for the 41 acres before purchasing it privately for £1,650.

A rear view of Grey Gutter Farm, Liverpool Road and some family members. The farm was demolished in 1962 to enable the road to be straightened

Thornton Farm, Liverpool Road

This large double-fronted farm house had 2 sitting rooms, 4 bedrooms and a hand-worked water pump over a well near the back door.. The farm buildings consisted of a double shippon for 10 cows, a two-stall cart horse stable with a loft above, a pig cote and hen roost. In 1906 the tenants, who were the executors of the late Thomas Yates, paid a rent of £19.5s and a tithe rent of 10s. 2 d for the 2 acres 3 roods and 7 perches farm. The family also worked some ground on the mere. After the farm was sold in 1906 for £600, it was the home of the Ashcroft family for many years. During the 1930s ice cream, made on the farm, was sold at the door.

Folly Farm – later known as 'Holly Farm'

The farm was situated at the end of Folly Lane and from 1851 to 1881 was tenanted by Edward Bridge who, in 1872, paid a rent of £217.14.8d for the 91 acres. According to the family, Mrs Margaret Ashcroft, the tenant, changed the name from *'Folly Farm'* to *'Holly Farm'* because she did not like the name.

This was obviously after 1901 when the census showed it as *'Folly Farm'*. It also had this name in 1851, 1861 and 1881.

The Ashcroft family outside their home, Holly Farm, which was at one time known as *'Folly Farm'*

Baldwin's Farm, Sluice Lane

The property was originally one building until Mr Pickervance added an extension in 1855 when he and his family lived in one of the cottages and the Caunce family lived in the other. For some years this was the home of James Caunce, a game keeper on the Hesketh estate. Robert Sharrock and Thomas Lea were the tenants in 1906 when the 15 acres, 3 perches farm was sold for £1,260 to Peter Freeman from Ormskirk. A Robert Pickavance, who worked on the railway, rented the semi detached property on the south side of the farm house and later purchased *'Wallflower Cottage'* (across the road) for his father William. He then built Roseacre Farm (house next door) for his own family. This farm and Wallflower Cottage are owned by Roberts grandsons, John and Robert. The two cottages of Baldwin's Farm have been extended and are now private houses.

Sluice Farm, Sluice Lane

This farm was situated over the bridge and on the right hand side of Sluice Lane and was thought to be the oldest inhabited home in the village, as old as the oldest part of Rufford Old

Hall (built 1530). It was a single storey, thatched property with stone *'garner'* steps on one end. (A *'garner'* was a granary or storage area). It had been the home of the Alty family for many years and it was from there that the son Richard married Ann Tootel, the daughter of Richard Tootel on 17 November 1672. Their great grandson, Richard, born in 1745 married Elizabeth Almond in 1768 and they lived at Bridge End Farm, Croston but sadly he drowned in the River Yarrow. Henry Alty, who married Isabella Strange in 1816, was the tenant in 1851 and when Henry died, Isabella tenanted the 45 acres farm, paying £82 annual rent in 1872. In 1808, a descendent Mary Alty, married the Rev Thomas Clarke, curate at St Mary's church. When the estate was sold in 1906 the farm house was still thatched and Messrs Sharrock and Lea were the tenants. The land was divided: some was added to Causeway Farm and some to Brick Kiln Farm

Causeway End Farm, Causeway Lane
The farm, so called because of its position at the Burscough end of the *'Causeway '*, had been tenanted for many years by the Martland family and in 1872 John Martland paid £200 annual rent for the 80 acres farm. When Sluice Farm and its buildings were demolished and the farm was broken up, some of the ground was added to Causeway Farm following the estate sale in 1906. At the beginning of the 20th century the farm, which consisted of a commodious farmhouse, farm buildings, an orchard and a thatched cottage, was tenanted by James Martland Ltd, agricultural merchants and farmers. Joe Aspinall was the foreman in 1944.

Cousins Farm, Cousins Lane
The tithe map of 1839 shows that the brick and slate farm house, farm buildings and 25 acres were tenanted by the family of John Caunce. In 1919 the farm was purchased by Martlands Ltd who later sold some of the land to *'Ormskirk*

Urban District Council', now the *'West Lancashire District Council'*. They built the first semi- detached houses in 1951 and the bungalows for rent in the 1960s. In the 1940s a pig farmer, Mr McKew, owned the original farm house and in the late 1960s the owners were Mr and Mrs Harris who used it as a fruit and vegetable shop. The much-altered farm house is still on the site.

Brick Kiln Farm, Brick Kiln Lane

Clay was dug from the many *'marl'* pits in the area to make bricks on the Hesketh estate. A map of 1763 shows that there was a *'brick kiln yard'* and a *'brick kiln hey'* (a plot of ground) on what is now known as *'Brick Kiln Lane.'*

Taken in 1905.this shows the cottages on Brick Kiln Lanc looking towards the village with Brick Kiln Farm on the right.

When builders were working in the loft of the farm house in the late 1990s they found white washed attic walls and traces of thatch which suggested that the property had been built in the 1700s and that the lofts had been used as accommodation. The farm house had six bedrooms until it was divided into two dwellings in 1906. Attached buildings were converted into two cottages. The roofs were covered with stone slabs until the 1960s when they were replaced by slate tiles. The complex now consists of a farm house, three cottages and a single store house that was converted from the *'Paddy House'*. This was also known as a *'shant'* and was used as accommodation for the Irish farm labourers who came over to harvest the potatoes until the 1950s. They worked on *'piece work'* (where people were paid for the amount of work done) and were paid in *'tallies'* (a brass disc with the name Martland stamped on). One tally was paid for each *'score'* worked (1 score equalled 20 yards) and they were exchanged for money at the end of the week. The Martland family purchased the farm from the Hesketh estate at the 1906 auction. They also purchased *'Sluice Farm'*, *'Causeway Farm'* and *'Tootle Cottage'* which was situated on the left at the corner of Tootle Lane, Mere Lane and Curlew Lane. It was then demolished but it had been the home of Mr W Caunce.

One of the longest serving agricultural labourers was a Rufford man, William Caunce. William started work at the farm in 1910 (as a *'teamsman'*- a man who worked with a team of horses) and during World War 1, he served in the Manchester regiment in France where he was gassed before being discharged home. In 1962, he received a long service medal from the Royal Agricultural Society for his 52 years service. He married Ada Ackers from Lathom and they lived at *'Burnley Cottage'*, Cousins Lane.

The farm was sold for £5,500 in November 1906.

A rent of £217.10s was paid for the 100acres, 2roods, 38 perches farm by various tenants, including Hugh Sharrock (1839,) James Alty (1851), John Ashcroft (1881) and Miss Elizabeth Ashcroft in (1906).

Mere End Farm, Tootle Lane
This farm was so called as it was situated at the eastern end of Martin Mere. The acreage was 85 acres, 1 rood and 10 perches and the farm was tenanted by Henry Bridge from 1851 to 1881

and by his widow Mary Bridge in 1901. By 1906, Mr and Mrs Thomas Prescott had moved from *'Tootle House Farm'* to farm at *'Mere End'* and they were followed by their 2 sons James and Thomas. *'Birch Hall'*, previously a single storey, wattle and daub building, was a workman's cottage belonging to the farm, therefore called *'tied'* as the occupant was tied to the owner..

A wedding day in 1929 at Mere End Farm with Dick Sephton on the left and his taxi driver.

Tootle House Farm, Tootle Lane
The house and farm building were built in the late 17th century at a place where three small creeks drained into Martin Mere. Some of the tenant farmers were Mrs Alice Halsall in 1839; Charles Yates in 1851(he had moved to the village from Scarisbrick); Mrs Ann Yates in 1872 (when she paid £126 per annum to rent 86 acres), James Prescott in 1901 (his son Thomas was born there before the family moved to Mere End Farm) and William Bridge in 1906. The 67 acres, 0 roods and 21 perches farm was not sold in the auction of 1906 but was sold for £1.700 in the later sale of 1920. The tenants at the time were Hugh Prescott and Harry Caunce.

In 1946 the farm was bought by Mr Hadfield who rented it to Henry Rimmer, nick-named *'Tracky'* because of his love of working with tractors while employed at *'Berry House Farm'* in Holmeswood.

Helm House Farm, Mere Lane

'Helm' is said to mean a *'cattle enclose'* and the original, undated wattle and daub cottage was where the *'scorer'* lived. He was the man (employed by the landowning Heskeths) who counted and recorded the names of the owners and the number of cattle that grazed on the mere during the drier summer months. The original Mere Lane was built along the side of a natural water gully. At the time of the Hesketh estate sale in 1906, the farm covered 25 acres, 3 roods and 12 perches and consisted of a thatched cart shed, poultry house and a shed for the young stock at a rent of £47. In the early 20th century the tenant was James Cheetham, followed in 1919 by Mr C Caunce.

Mere Farm, Mere Lane

This was a smallholding with a timber-built house and was situated on the right side of Mere Lane and near to the sluice bank. An un-named Canadian man known locally as *'the Canadian'* lived there in the1930s before Thomas Chadwick, who lived there in about 1948 before he moved to live in Sandy Way, Holmeswood. The buildings were demolished and there are now no visible remains.

TRADES AND CRAFTS

At the time of the Domesday Book, 1086, this region was an area of poverty but changed to a more prosperous economy in the 13th and 14th centuries with the emergence of markets and fairs, e.g. Rufford market and fair in 1339 and with the supplying of locally grown produce to the towns of Liverpool, Preston and Wigan.

The majority of Rufford people worked in agriculture, but many worked in other trades and crafts.

In 1906, the historian and rector of Rufford Rev WG Proctor gathered information from the Parish Register, the Parish Account Book and other documents concerning the history of Rufford, its church and its people. The documents identified that in 1646, William Baron, who lived in a cottage near to *'the Cunnery'*, was a carpenter and that between 1730 and 1743 there were weaving looms in at least 12 cottages. One was the home of Robert Hesketh and his wife Catherine who were *'stuff'* weavers.(woollen cloth or fabric) There were also six shoemakers, one clogger (called *'Leather'* Barton), a chair maker, a saddler, a saddle-tree maker (man who made the frame for a saddle), four shop keepers, four inkeepers, a miller, a potato *'badger'*(a man who bought and sold potatoes), a potato *'swaler'*(a dealer or middle man of today), two carpenters, two wheelwrights, two blacksmiths (one being Evan Caunce), a mason and brick setter (John Porter),two butchers, a *'webber'* (a male weaver),and a *'maltster'*(a man who makes or deals in malt for the brewing of beer). The son of the previously mentioned Robert and Catherine Hesketh was a maltster and the family lived in a house near to *'Shrub House'* where there was an adjoining malt house. In 1802 Lewis Ashurst (a freemason) was a maltster and in 1824 Thomas Norris carried on this trade. Following the enforcement of the *'Shop Tax'*, 1785-1789, four shops in Rufford

47

paid tax but this excluded small shops that did not pay church or poor rates.

By the end of the 18th century the canal had been cut and new trades emerged. These included an *'excise man'* (who collected duty on commodities or on various licences), a *'sails man'* (possibly someone who worked on the *'coastal flats'* boats that had flat bottoms and small sails. These were used when they reached the Irish Sea at Preston after sailing along the Rufford branch and the River Douglas) and a *'boat man'* (the person in charge of a hired boat).

Other names and occupations that were recorded for 1824 were; Richard Dandy - *shopkeeper*, Charles Dandy- *surgeon* and William Dandy - *joiner*.

In 1688 a man was buried in the churchyard and the words *'Oat bread'* Mason were engraved on his tombstone. It is likely that Mr Mason was a baker.

To enable youngsters to have a trade, the Hesketh estate had an apprentice scheme called *'The Rufford Apprentice Register'* which showed that on 31 December 1805, Thomas Stopforth, aged 8 years, son of Mary Stopforth, was apprenticed to Edward Ashcroft, a Rufford farmer.

With the completion of the railway and with the progression of time, many new occupations were recorded in the 1881 census. John Bradshaw was the *'station master'*, Henry Stazicker a *'railway porter'*, Thomas Kerfoot a *'plate layer'*, Richard Barron the *'parish clerk'*, Peter Caunce a *'coal merchant'* and Thomas Hopkirk a *'land agent'*. By this time there was also a Methodist preacher. Some of the trades and professions recorded in the 1891 census were ' *boot and shoe makers'*, a *'basket maker'*, a' *printer*, two *'joiners'*, a *'paviour'* (a man who paved with flag stones or cobbles), ten *'dress makers'*, two *'teachers'*, two *'school mistresses'*, a *'sick nurse'* , a *'solicitor's clerk'*, two *'insurance agents'*, a *'governess'*, a *'children's nurse'*, a *'pork butcher'*, four *'grocers'*, an *'ostler'* (he looked after horses), a *'miller'* and two *'publicans'*.

The 1901 census showed that the majority of men were still employed as agricultural labourers but at least fifteen were employed on the railway; four *'railway clerks'*, four *'platelayers'*, four *'porters'*, one *'labourer'*, one *'signalman'* and one *'station master'*. Some other occupations included two *'wheelwrights,* two *'blacksmiths'*, two *'inn keepers'*, three *'coal merchants'*, three *'grocers'*, three *'brick layers'*, a *'basket maker'*, *'miller'*, *'fire man'*, *'boot and shoemaker'*, *'seamstress'*, *'dressmaker'* and two *'corn merchants'*.(The fire man was probably a *'boiler tenter'* or a railway fireman, not a fire fighter.

EDUCATION

When the first chapel was endowed in 1347 during the time of Sir William Hesketh, one of the duties of the clergyman was to teach the children of Rufford. All through the Dark Ages, from Edward III (1327-1377) to Henry VIII (1509-1547) the church and the lord of the manor did something in the way of education. The chantry priests were the first school masters. The priests were probably not members of an order but were of the old faith (Roman Catholic Church) and paid by the Heskeths. It was not known where these schools were held but old maps show a plot of land called *'priests acre'* where there had possibly been a house or residence of a clergyman and, as its name suggests, *'Hermitage Farm'* was also a possible site. Some ministers who acted as schoolmasters were Rev Bradshaw (1610), Rev William Wood (1650) and Rev Edward Atherton (1706). Some of the 18th century school masters were John Whiteside (1738) Edward Forshaw (1768) Thomas Driver (1775) and James Fazackerly (1776).

A class at Rufford school in the early 1920's with a young Stanley Lingard in the centre front

School photograph taken in July 1947
Back-Tom Smith, John Smith, Keith Halton, Mrs Edge Standing-Michael
Bamber, David Colling, Sheila Jones,Audrey Halton, Winnie Sharrot, Cedric
Demaine, Ernest Croskell, Sitting-Wendy Clayton, Betty Sharrot, Maureen
Rawsthorne, Stella Ashcroft. Babs Sullivan,Maureen Ritchie, Front- Derek
Watkinson, Brian Martland, John Caulfield, Jack Greenwood.

The first direct mention of a school or school master was when
Sir Thomas Hesketh (1465-1523) left money in his will for the
erection of *'alms houses and a school for Rufforthe'*. This school
was destroyed at the same time as the chantry in the church,
and another school, managed by the rector of Croston and Mrs
Bellingham (a relative of Sir Thomas Hesketh) was established
in 1712, probably in an outbuilding at the Old Hall. In 1816
when the Lowe family tenanted the Old Hall, Sir Thomas
Dalrymple Hesketh repaired the upstairs with the purpose of
making a school to supersede the one built in 1712. Later the
school moved to the curate's lodgings at *'Sluice Farm'*.
The girls' school was held in *'Rosebank Cottage'* Flash Lane,
which was built in 1675. This building was divided into two;
one part used as the school room and the other the home of
the mistress. This cottage continued to be used as the girls'
school house and in 1824 Sir Thomas Dalrymple Hesketh built

the present school for boys. The Rev R Pearson was appointed school master to the 13 children on the condition that he appointed a competent assistant.

In 1833 the school was open for lessons on 3 weekdays plus Sunday. The old girls' school then became the Hesketh estate office where a larger than average letter box was made in the door to enable tenants to post their paperwork. An agreement was made between Sir Thomas and another school master, Robert Abbott, about the cost of the education. The charge was 3 shillings per quarter year for the farmers' children and no more than one penny per week for the children of estate workers.

Mr Abbott was a man of many talents. Along with his role as school master, he also collected taxes, had charge of the public weigh machine, was one time postmaster, vestry clerk, clerk to the parish council and wrote wills for the villagers. When there was a funeral or sale in the village, the children had a day's holiday from school to enable Mr Abbott to read the will or to act as clerk or cashier. He had a sad personal life due mainly to his wayward son, John, who had been in the Coldstream Guards and fought in the Crimean War. Following discharge from the army, John died in the Lancaster Lunatic Asylum and his father retired to live in Preston where he died aged 80 years. He is buried in Rufford churchyard.

In 1909 there was an outbreak of measles and the school was closed for 3 weeks. During the summer holidays the bare brick walls in the school were plastered and during the same year the 'Peter Lathom Charity' gave bank books plus a deposit to every child to encourage them to save money.

For many years the school held an annual 'Summer Gala'. In 1910 the weather was glorious and the procession, headed by the Rufford band, went through the village and called at the Old and New Halls. The villagers then had tea in the school before going to the park where the children were reported to have had a grand time with bats and balls, skipping ropes and races.

In the same year a son and heir was born to Mr and Mrs Fermor Hesketh and, to celebrate the event, the school children collected £32.15s.4d which was donated to Dr Barnardo's Homes.

Further Education
Education at the time did not stop at school age. The report of the Director of Technical Instruction at Lancashire County Council, 1891-1892, identified that Rufford people attended lectures on poultry, horticulture, beekeeping and management of farm stock. The fee was two pence per lecture but the beekeeping class was free. During the same period twenty six people attended the cookery lectures. In 1907, handbills were circulated around the village to inform people about the proposed Lancashire County Council Education Committee's evening classes which were to be held in the school. The take-up rate was obviously not high because two years later another handbill was distributed to try to encourage more people to attend. In the parish magazine of 1910 it was stated that only five youths (two from outside of the village) were attending and *"the girls are no better!"*

CHURCHES AND CHARITIES

Parish Church of St Mary The Virgin, Rufford with Holmeswood

It is impossible to say when the first church or chapel was built on the site of the present church, but the Rev. WT Bulpit in his book *'Notes on Southport and District'* (1908), said that a church, probably older than the one at Rufford, had stood in the Chapel Field, Holmeswood. This site was to the south of Holmeswood Hall and overlooked Martin Mere. The mid-Victorian writer, Rev Raines said that a chapel existed in Rufford before the reign of Edward III (1327-1377).

The Church of 1346

As a thanksgiving for his safe return from the wars in France, Sir William De Heskaith endowed a chantry (a small chapel within a church) in the chapel in Rufford in 1352. Two further chantries were endowed at Rufford, one to Alice Hesketh in 1495 and Thomas Hesketh in 1523. Priests, usually poorly paid, were appointed to chant services for the welfare of individuals or for the souls of the dead. The Hesketh family kept the chapel in good repair and in 1522 they added a steeple that housed four bells.

During the Civil War (1642-1651), many of the sculptures, carvings and stained glass were destroyed. The only things that remain from this chapel are two moulded capitals now placed either side of the present church porch and an alabaster slab on the floor in the Hesketh chapel. This is dedicated to Thomas Hesketh (died 1463), his wife Margaret and their eleven children.

It was noted in papers discovered by Rev Procter when he came to Rufford in 1906, that Thomas Baldwin and Henry Jackson had spent a large amount of money on refreshments while bargaining for a new Communion table in 1681. The cost of drinks had featured largely in all account records as no parish business had been conducted without people *'wetting their whistles'*.

The Church of 1734

Rufford constituted part of the parish of Croston until 1793 when it and Chorley became independent parishes with Rev Richard Masters as Rufford's first rector. A 1650 Parliamentary recommendation to separate the two parishes had failed.

The Hesketh family rebuilt the chapel again in 1734 at a cost of £1,165. It was described by the historian Edward Baines as *'a plain brick edifice with a neat and even elegant interior'* while Bulpit saw it as *'a plain, heavy, barn like structure'*. The building obviously had a first floor gallery because on January 4th 1736, the rector Rev E Grey gave permission for Edward Halsall, an innkeeper, to rent gallery pew number 5 for an annual charge of £5. A new organ was purchased in 1847 to replace the previous one that had been worked by hand.

In 1817, under the direction of William Shakeshaft (land agent), vaults were built under the chancel and the tomb of Lady Sophie Hesketh , who had recently died, and the tomb of Sir Thomas Hesketh who had died in 1782, were placed there.

In the 15th century, Thomas the son of Robert and Dame Alice Hesketh had left money in his will for the erection of a stone wall around the church yard. It was not until 1825 that James Robinson built the wall at a cost of £107.25s.10d. The wall stretched from *'the muchine house'* (exact site unknown) and along Chapel Road as far as the garden of *'Church Farm'* that was then tenanted by Robert Alty. There was originally a small gate in the wall at the eastern end of the church yard.

The 1734 church which was built at a cost of £1,165 and described by Bulpit as a *'barn like structure'* The side entrance is on the left but was this originally designed to be further to the right?

The iron railings along the south side of the churchyard were erected when Diamond Jubilee Road was made in 1897 to celebrate the sixtieth anniversary of Queen Victoria's accession to the throne. There was a new gate from the churchyard onto the road and the original gate in the wall was bricked up. The name and date of this new road are carved into the coping stones of the wall at the side of *'Church Farm'*, now called *'Manor Farm'*.

The 1869 Church

The present Gothic-styled building was built in 1869 at a cost of £5000 that was funded by public subscription. It was designed by architects Messrs Danson and Davies of Liverpool and built in red brick and sandstone. The steeple contains two bells. One had been used in the previous church and was made by Luke Ashton of Wigan in 1746 and the second bell was made by Taylors of Loughborough in 1863. Although one bell is cracked, they are both used on special occasions.

When permission was granted to rebuild the church, some of the old graves were dug up and the remains moved to the outside of the church. The new walls were built on the outside of the old church and in 1871; the church was closed for two years to enable the old walls to be removed. During this time, services were held in the school until the church was re-consecrated in May 1873. The church was gradually completed over the following years and the pews were added in 1894-5.

Rev Bulpit described the church as being *'very handsome'* and it contains many fine artefacts including the marble wall plaque, sculptured by Flaxman at a cost of £800. This is a figure of *'Hope'* holding an anchor and commemorates Sophie Hesketh who died in 1817. There are stained glass windows, a pulpit made of Caen stone, a polished granite font (a masonic gift in memory of Sir Thomas Fermor Hesketh who died in 1872), an 18th century charity board, a glass case containing a bassoon used in the church orchestra, brass wall plaques, some 18th century floor tiles, the font from the 18th century church, a brass chandelier and a painting of the Royal Arms, both dated 1763.

St Mary's church taken about 1910 from the canal bridge and showing the small gate into the churchyard. This was needed for access before Diamond Jubilee Road was made in 1897.

The 1869 church at the beginning of the 20th century with visitors dressed in the fashion of the time.

The church was lit by carbide gas and oil lights until the installation of electricity about 1925 and an electric fan blower for the organ resulted in the redundancy of the manual bellow and of the man who had to pump them by hand. The church accounts of 1908 showed that Thomas Bridge *'the organ blower'* was paid an annual salary of one pound five shillings.

A bricked up door arch was recently found in the *'blowers'chamber'* behind the organ and suggestions are that there was a possible entry into the cellar from inside the church.

The churchyard (God's Acre)

In the parish magazine of June 1906, the rector wrote that he was concerned about the state of the church yard and said *'it should be the most beautiful and best cared for spot in the whole village'*. With the help of volunteers and voluntary contributions from parishioners, the site was cleared up and tidied. (For some years there was a male urinal sited in the south-east corner of the church yard!)

In 1853, a licence was granted to Isabella Boosie to bury her late husband David in unconsecrated ground. Sir Thomas George Hesketh approved an extension to the church yard in 1853 and this was consecrated later the same year.

The base of the old preaching cross, dated AD1000, can be seen today on the south side of the church yard and is the oldest dated item in the village. A more modern cross was erected in 1888 as a memorial to the people whose graves were disturbed when the present church was built.

There are many 17th century graves. The oldest has the date 1632 and the initials T.A. (Thomas Ashcroft). Some of the gravestones also identify the occupation of the deceased, e.g. *Richard Alty-bassoon* and *James Culshaw-wheelwright*. Three previous rectors are buried here, Rev E Atherton who died in 1706, Rev J F Hogg-Goggins who died in 1905 and Rev W G Proctor who died in 1911.

The base of the old preaching cross of AD 1000 with the first sundial, dedicated in July 1909. This was later stolen and replaced by one dedicated to the late Margaret Ashcroft.

A sundial (later stolen) was erected on the base of the old preaching cross and was dedicated on July 14 1909 by the Rev Proctor. The pillar was part of the old font from the 1736 church and the brass dial, dated 1670, was purchased by the rector in Manchester. This was later stolen and never recovered.

In 2004, a new sundial, dedicated to Margaret Ashcroft of Fearns Farm, Rufford, was erected in the base of the old cross. The inscription, "a *treasured Christian lady whose life was dedicated to the serving of others*", is around the base. Margaret was the organiser of the *'Girls Friendly Society'*, a fundraiser and life-long worshipper at the church.

The New Burial Ground

When the old church yard was full, a new burial ground was made in the grounds of the old rectory that had been situated across from the church in Church Road. With the co-operation and willingness of many local men, the laborious task of digging up tree stumps from the old orchard and the making of the new burial ground was completed in 1930. The leader of this *'fine communal enterprise'* was John Lea who died in 1940 aged 83 years. Although he was buried in the old church yard, he also had a fitting epitaph in the new extension to

'God's Acre'. A stone slab set into the pathway was inscribed *'J.L. 1930'.*
When the new churchyard was completed, a friend of Rev McGrath wrote the following lines;

Folk say the men of England
Can't work as men of old,
But these true men of Rufford
Give lie to what is told.
With their fine leader they have shown,
As men did in the past,
That when good work is wanted done
These Rufford men stand fast.
Until all labour's ended
And each man's work is done
Then to this sacred piece of land
Each one in turn will come.

Garden of Remembrance
When cremations became an alternative to burial, a village facility was needed to enable people to bury the ashes of their loved ones. In 1982, the *'Garden of Remembrance'* was created between Church Road and the new burial ground.

Rector and curates of St Mary's Church
There are 48 incumbents listed for the parish of Rufford beginning with the abbots of Chester in 1160 and finishing with the present rector, Canon Jim Burns. Rufford had been part of the parish of Croston and when a separate parish was formed in 1793, the first rector was Rev Edward Masters. Although he had the living for more than 40 years, he did not concern himself with parish affairs, had no house in Rufford but lived in Tarleton and (later) Hesketh Bank. Canon Chamberlain came in 1843 and lived in Rufford Old Hall until 1848 when he moved to the former home of estate land agent

61

David Boosie. That house was used as the rectory for many years until it was demolished in 1927. It was always known as *'the old rectory'* and was on Church Road opposite the church and to the right of the present rectory.

Lord Freddie Hesketh laying the foundation stone for the new rectory in July 1949.
Church House Farm is on the left.

The foundation stone for the new rectory was laid in 1949 by Lord Freddie Hesketh. Rev Goggin was appointed in 1868, and as he suffered from rheumatism, he found the rectory damp and unhealthy. When he was unable to purchase building land in Rufford, he moved to live in Churchtown and visited Rufford weekly before he moved again to live in Bretherton. He took the additional surname of Hogg in 1884. Rev Proctor lived in the old rectory during his ministry 1905 - 1911.

Rev and Mrs Hall were the next family to live in the old rectory but when they also experienced the damp conditions they purchased and lived at *'The Hermitage'* on Liverpool Road. When the old rectory was demolished and Rev Hall retired, Rev McGrath (1936-1941), lived first at *'The Elms'*, Holmeswood Road before moving to *'Red Cott'*, Liverpool Road. Whilst he was there, he changed the name to *'Apple Cottage'* and started the new rectory fund. The next two rectors, Smithies and Steinley also lived at *'Apple Cottage'* and when Rev Jones started his ministry in 1950, the new rectory had been built in Church Road. All subsequent ministers have lived at that address; Canon Mellor (1956), Rev Dewey (1960),

Rev Howson (1971), Rev Jones (1978), Rev Swann (1995) and Canon Burns from 2000.

Ormskirk Dissenting Meeting (Fogg's Chapel) -

A Presbyterian chapel, founded in 1784, is thought to have been at the corner of Aughton Street and Bridge Street in Ormskirk but the exact site is unknown. Around 1838, it was named *'Fogg's Chapel'* after the minister Rev Henry Fogg. It originated from a Congregational meeting at a former chapel in Chapel Street founded in 1696. The Presbyterian Church flourished in the 17th and 18th centuries but by the late 18th century many Presbyterian had adopted Unitarianism. The baptisms of three Rufford children were recorded in the register at 'Fogg's Chapel':- Ann, the daughter of John Radcliff was baptised on November 20th 1716 and George the son of Thomas Lowe on August 3rd 1777. An older son of Thomas and Elizabeth Lowe was baptised at Rufford Old Hall on 29th August 1775. Fogg's Chapel closed in 1886 and in 1972, the Presbyterian Church merged with the Congregational church to form the *'United Reform Church'*.

Congregational Union

This was created in the vestry of Mosley Street Chapel, Manchester in 1806 and a circular was issued concerning the formation of an *'Itinerant Society'*. Their first attempt at working in the community was in the western parts of Lancashire that included Rufford. In his book *'Lancashire Nonconformity'* (1893), the Rev B Nightingale stated that Rufford was *'an interesting state'* and was also *'a flourishing cause for a short time'*.

The Society of Friends (Quakers)

Although the nearest Quaker burial ground was in Graveyard Lane, Bickerstaffe (it had been purchased in 1665 with the last burial being in 1813), there were no Rufford people buried there, though, in 1662, a Rufford man, William Thompson, was prosecuted for teaching in a private house during the prolonged and bitter persecution of Quakers during the 17th century.

Roman Catholicism

It was after St Augustine arrived in Britain that the pagan English were converted to the Roman Catholic faith. Following the Protestant Reformation in the 16th century the majority of the people conformed to the teachings of the Church of England and only a minority remained loyal to the Roman Catholic faith. During the Elizabethan period (1558-1603) the Heskeths still had Roman Catholic sympathies but outwardly they conformed to Church of England practices. Alice (nee Holcroft) wife of Sir Thomas Hesketh (1526-1588) and most of her children were practising Catholics but her eldest son Robert (1560-1620) decided to conform. Masses were often said in the large houses in the area where there was often a secret room for the priest to hide. The secret chamber in Rufford Old Hall was *'the priest's hole'* where a Latin service book was found on the floor. In the 1580s Rev Worthington, a Catholic priest had found a safe haven there. Priests also masqueraded as *'ordinary people'*. The list of Papists and Reputed Papists for the township of Rufford in 1767 identified five adults and eight children. These included John Smith, a blacksmith, John Roscow, a labourer, Frances, wife of John Draper and Mary, wife of James Forshaw.

Ruffords Roman Catholics have had to travel to churches in Burscough, Mawdesley and Tarleton.

Methodism

John Wesley 1703-1791, the British founder of Methodism had converted from the Church of England to evangelism in 1738 and toured the country on horseback, preaching in the open air. He preached one sermon from the preaching cross on the village green in Rufford, but had sensed a wickedness about the place and wept when he left. A villager, Jane Caunce had heard the sermon and related this to Edward Bridge 40 years later.

Edward Bridge (1774-1855) was the first Rufford person to be associated with Methodism. At 21 years of age, he went to Lancaster as a bodyguard to Sir Thomas Dalrymple Hesketh. While there, he heard a group of singers who were later identified to him as 'Methodists'. Although he had been a church warden from 1834 to 1835, he became a disciple of Wesley.

In April 1809, Rev Benjamin Wood and Rev. Joseph Hollingwood preached in a barn at Holmes (Tarleton) and the service was attended by Edward Bridge and his relatives. They invited the two preachers to visit 'Lane End Farm', Rufford, the home of the Bridge family. The two men preached under the pear tree that grew against the farmhouse and In the nearby barn. The fruit from the tree was sold to fund missionary work. Inside the barn, the floor was strewn with straw for the Saturday services and Sunday school. These services continued for the next 60 years.

Despite the fact that in 1810 the local curate preached a sermon on 'the pernicious weed of Methodism', by 1811 there were 30 members, one of whom was John Pickavant, the son of the village shoemaker, a regular attendee from the time of the first service.

Between visiting the sick and running his farm, Edward Bridge invented various agricultural implements including his 'ploughing-down plough' for use between the drills of potatoes. The plough was loaned to other villagers but people from outside the village, who referred to it as the 'Methody plough', were refused.

Looking down a cobbled Brick Kiln Lane from the village with the Methodist chapel on the left. The thatched cottage on the right was the site of a later cottagefrom which sweets were sold.

Brick Kiln Lane with Wayside Cottages on the left, the Methodist chapel on the right and the entrance to Brick Kiln Farm in the foreground.

Following the death of Edward Bridge, who was known as '*the Hero of Rufford*', his daughter, Jane Moss, ('*Mother Moss*') opened her cottage in Brick Kiln Lane for services and baptisms.

The first two entries in the *'Register of Baptisms'* for baptisms at the cottage were Margaret Jane, daughter of Richard and Mary Hesketh and Elizabeth, daughter of Thomas and Elizabeth Sharrock. The son of James and Jane Blundell was christened on Christmas Day 1879.

The site of the present chapel was purchased from Sir Thomas George Hesketh and the foundation stone was laid by Thomas Bridge of Burscough on May 28th 1879. The chapel was opened in 1881 and the last service was held in 1989. The building was altered and opened on 12th May 1990 as the *'Rufford Centre'*, a Methodist Retreat that provides a place of seclusion for religious exercises. Services were and still are held in the former Sunday School building at the rear. The chapel belongs to the Ormskirk circuit and visiting clergy and lay speakers preach at the weekly service.

Plymouth Brethren

At the end of the 19th century and into the 20th century, several Rufford families were members of this fundamentalist Christian sect, founded by the Rev John Darby in 1827. They were known locally as the *'Black Stockiners'* and their weekly meetings were held in a house down Brick Kiln Lane. They did not believe in having radios or newspapers and on Sundays they read the Bible and would not undertake any work or household tasks. When a sect member died, the funeral service was held in the meeting house before burial in the parish church yard.

Some of the local members were from a branch of a family, called Bolton.

Benefactors, Fundraising and Charities

From earliest times the people of Rufford have given and received monies. On 11th May 1662, the congregation of Rufford Chapel gave the sum of 4s. 6d. for the Protestant churches in Lithuania.

In the church there is a tablet, dated c.1745 that shows a list of donors and the amount of their donations. These include James Hesketh - £10, Oliver Tittington - £5, Jennet Hesketh - £8.10s, Thomas Baldwin - £20, Robert Turner - £10 and Richard Berry - £20.

'*The Rufford Clothing Club*' was set up to encourage thrift and in 1845, 38 men and five women contributed between one shilling and 4s.6d. per month to the fund. Lady Hesketh subscribed £10, Mrs Polk £2 and other benefactors £7. In one month, Mr Astle, the school master distributed £30.18s. The club had also distributed part of Peter Lathom's charity in the form of a bonus on subscriptions and although the clothing club still existed in1910, it is not known when it ceased. During the Second World War the activities of the '*Clothing Club*' were resumed to help villagers who were eligible for assistance under the original conditions. In 1940 it was known as the '*Rufford and Holmeswood Clothing Club*'.

An article in the 15th October 1857 edition of the '*Ormskirk Advertiser*' stated that William and Robert Halliwell collected £17.5s in a house to house collection for the '*Indian Relief Fund*'. The fund was to relieve the suffering of fellow country men and women in India and the article said that "*Rufford people set a patriotic example by their giving*".

In 1859 the same paper published an article on the establishment of a '*Penny Bank*' for the villagers of Rufford . Sir Thomas Hesketh had donated £1 and Rev Thomas Foster Chamberlain had given 10sh to purchase books for the bank. Subscriptions were collected weekly and any deposit of between one penny and five shillings attracted an interest rate of two and a half percent if the money was left in the account for 6 months.

The '*Overseers Relief Book*' of 1867 (now in the Lancashire Record Office,) showed that some villagers had been in receipt of loans and donations. The family of James Berry had received 14s.5d while he was serving in the militia, Ellen

68

Wignall received 24 shillings to hire a pair of weaving looms, her husband Robert received 10 shillings for a scythe and John Lea was loaned £5 to buy a new mangle.

A new church organ was installed in 1867 at a cost of £800. and when the rector printed a list of donations to the *'New Organ Fund'*, money had been donated from the harvest thanksgiving in 1885. Among the first organists were Richard Smith, James Hurst and Mr Webb, the school master.

A cycle parade and athletic sports event were held on Saturday 15th June 1912 to raise money for the *'Church Decoration Fund'*. The event included a procession through the village, weight lifting, maypole dancing, an exhibition by the boy scouts, firework display, donkey races, cycle parade and refreshments

On July 2nd 1925 a *'Grand Fete and Bazaar'* was held on Rufford Park to raise funds for the parish church and school. Additional funds were raised on the same day when Dr Petyt, who had a practice at the *'Mansion House'* in Longton and lived adjacent to the park at *'Rose Cottage'*, opened his garden to the public at a cost of 6d per person. ('Rose *Cottage'* was later known as *'The Chase'*: the 5 ¾ acres plot was sold for £2,250. at the 1906 sale).

'Rose Cottage'. Flash Lane,The home of Dr Petyt who opened his garden to raise money for the parish church. The property is now called *'The Chase'*.

In his 1710 will, Dr Layfield, rector of Croston, left one quarter of his estate to assist the poor in several parishes in the area, including Rufford. *'The Layfield Trust'* still exists.
Peter Lathom, from Bispham, left money in his 1700 will for the benefit of the needy in Rufford and in 16 other villages in south-west Lancashire. Money was donated for clubs, prizes for education, bedding, tools, coal and food or families. Today, donations of money are distributed among villagers.

In 1745, two Rufford men, Baldwin and Berry, gave £20 each to be distributed to the poor of the village on 21st December, St Thomas' Day. The charity was   discontinued about 1815.

PUBLIC HOUSES

Between 1758 and 1791 the *'Rufford Parish Register'* recorded the occupation of ten men as *'innkeepers'*. They were Edward Halsall, Thomas Alty, Edward Usher, James Forshaw, Thomas Norris, Thomas Barron, Thomas Abram, Edward Hailwood and William Bramwell. The names of William Bramwell and Thomas Norris were on the list of *'Alehouse Recognizance'* (a list of people who were licensed to run a public house) for the year 1780. Between 1841 an 1861 there was only one innkeeper recorded but by 1881 this had increased to two.

The Fermor Arms Hotel, Station Road

The name *'Fermor'* was added to that of *'Hesketh'* when the Hesketh family inherited the Fermor estate at Easton Neston, in Northamptonshire after the marriage of Sir Thomas George Hesketh and Lady Anna Maria Arabella Fermor in 1846.

The Inn after the top storey had been removed because the building had been built in a foundation of cotton bales. The clock was a dominant feature. The vehicle is a Mini Traveller, and helps date the picture to the 1960's.

71

The original three storey inn before the top storey was removed along with the farm buildings on the left.

When the hotel was built in the early 1870s as a coaching house for railway and canal workers, it was described as a *'newly built and gigantic building'*. It was surrounded by fields and was part of a working farm. From 1870 to 1892 the landlord was Robert Ashcroft. It was originally a three-storey building built on a foundation of cotton bales and in later years, when the building began to subside, the upper storey was removed. Tom Lyon was the landlord in 1901 and he allowed the village youngsters to use part of the old farm buildings as a social club. This club room, over a horse loose box, was 59 ft 6 in x 17ft and included a serving room. During World War 2, Mrs Culshaw had a café over the stables and the facilities also included a bowling green and a tennis court. The two-storey building was later demolished and replaced in 1974 by the single storey *'New Fermor Arms'* which closed in 1992. The owners of this pub, the Mawdesley brothers, sold their home brewed beer called '*Fettlers Ale*'. When the New Fermor closed, the building was converted into a residential care home '*Alsley Lodge*'.

The Hesketh Arms Inn

The inn was built as a coaching house and dates from the late 1700s. It was set in a 9-acre site and included a brew house, stabling for 12 horses, many outbuildings and a weighbridge which was sited across the road. (This was only capable of weighing loads on two- wheeled carts and ceased to be used by the early 1900s). The two-storey extension to the left included a dining room for travellers using the Liverpool to Preston turnpike road which opened in 1770.

In the early 1800s when Richard Worthington was the landlord, the building had 40 windows but when the tenancy changed, the new landlord bricked up ten and reduced the '*Window Tax*' to £9.16.3d. Business between the church and the Hesketh Arms was obviously brisk when Mr Alderson was landlord in 1817 because bills for drinks featured frequently in the parish church accounts.

Due to the difficulties in travelling to Croston, the jury of the Township of Rufford used an upstairs room in the inn as a court room. On 2nd June 1822, they assembled at 9am to discuss the state of the water courses and the boundaries.

Taken in 1907 before the building on the right was demolished. The iron railings were removed to smelt down during the First World War.

From the early 20th century many of the outbuildings were used for a variety of village functions. One large shed (known as '*the tent*') had seating for 400 people and was used for social gatherings while the inn was used for the weekly brass band practices and for the annual *'Pot fair'*. There was a bowling green, petrol pumps, a chip shop, and a betting shop. Silcock's fair was held annually in the ground, and in later years the local pigeon club met in an outbuilding.

Some former landlords were Mary Barron (1851), Henry Hurst (1866), Philip Ascroft (1881) and Henry Hurst (1891). A later manager was Mr Haymer who came from Liverpool with his family. A Rufford man, Jack Ratcliffe married the daughter and he kept pigs and poultry in a building behind the inn.

The Spread Eagle Tavern

This wayside inn was built in the 16th century and was situated at the junction of Preston Road and the road that led to Holmeswood, now Flash Lane. At that time, it was the principal tavern in the village and had the sign of the spread eagle (the Hesketh family crest) over the door. It was described as being *"picturesque, thatched and superior in size and accommodation to any other building in the village"*. The entry was via a low porch. Clean floor rushes and a good fire offered cheer and comfort to customers.

Looking up Flash Lane from Liverpool Road with the old schoolhouse on the left and *'Ivy Cottage'* on the right. This was formerly *'The Spread Eagle Inn'*.

One of the first landlords was Philipp Aassecrofte (an old spelling of Philip Ascroft), whose wife Janet was the daughter of Dick Wignall from Tarleton. The Register of Rufford recorded the death, on 29th February 1811, of Thomas Wilson, steward at the Spread Eagle and the tithe map of 1837 showed that William Hurst was the landlord.

By the beginning of the 20th century the inn had closed and the property became the home of Annie Walsh who sold home made ice-cream to visitors to the park.

The property is now a dwelling - '*Ivy Cottage*'.

The Swan Inn

The building was situated on the edge of '*the Moor*' on the outskirts of the village. Travellers were not encouraged to stay within the village because of local people's wariness of strangers. In 1760 the inn was part of a working farm. Water from the four wells on the site was used in the brew house which was a single-storey, thatched, lean-to with a large cellar. When the bedrooms were occupied by travellers, the family slept in the windowless attics where a later owner of the property had found the words '*Swan Inn*' scratched on a wall and traces of rushes that had been used to block up draughts in the walls.

The inn was on the site of the present smithy house and the former brew house is now used as a smithy. There was a door leading from the brew house into the stillage room next door. There are still slots in the walls at ground level where the beams were inserted into the wall for storing the barrels of ale. The central window in the front of the present building was the original entrance into the inn, which closed in the 1820s.

SOME OTHER BUILDINGS AND PLACES OF INTEREST

Throughout the centuries, the main road through the village has been known as *'Turnpike Road'*, *'Preston Road'* and *'Liverpool Road'* After being a turnpike, (privately funded road repaired from rates) it became free from tolls after 1835. In 1888 when Lancashire County Council was formed, it became known as a *'main road'* and became a *'trunk'* road in the 1920s. This was confirmed by an Act of Parliament in 1936. Some of the old buildings and places of interest are still to be seen, some have changed use and some have disappeared.

Beech House, Church Road
Built in 1736, the house was set in seven acres of land that included a large orchard (now *'Beech Close'*) and a 300 years old beech tree that is now under a preservation order. For many years it was the home of various employees of the Hesketh estate. They included David Boosie, factor for the estate in 1851, John Porter, land agent in 1881 and Thomas Hobkirk, a retired land agent in 1901. In 1891, two other families also lived on the site; William Baldwin an agricultural labourer and his family of six and John Bridge also a labourer, and his family of five, plus one lodger.

In the 20th century Mr Porter, a school governor lived there and he was followed by Mr Allen the village veterinary surgeon who was known to have owned the first motor car in Rufford. The stables, which had an entrance onto Church Road, were used to house large animals that needed treatment. Tom Hey, originally from Leyland, served his apprenticeship with Mr Allen before opening his own practice at the *'The Apiary'*, Holly Lane. Mr and Mrs Campbell, timber dealers from Liverpool, were the next owners of the property and they were followed by the Sherlocks. Over the years the yard and buildings have been converted and are known as *'The Stables'*

76

Church Road showing horse drawn vehicles,' *May Cottage'* the home of the village shoe maker on the left, and the entrance to *'Beech House'* stable on the right.

The Rookery

This small cottage was where the *'scorer'* lived. He was employed by the landlord to count the numbers and owners' names of cattle and sheep as they went to graze in the *'park'* which had previously been the private pleasure ground of the Hesketh family. Two gentlemen visiting Rufford in 1870, described the cottage as *'a compact little home , surrounded by tall elm trees, with a small front garden with four steps leading through the gate onto Preston Road, a square lawn and a cavernous well with a rough hewn stone cover'*. The 55 feet deep well was said to be the deepest in the village. In 1881, William Webb, the headmaster of the school lived there and in 1901 it was tenanted by James Alty. Following the sale of the estate in 1906, the property has had several owners.

The Hermitage (Liverpool Road)

The property had originally been built as a hostelry in the late 19th century and was purchased by Dr Henry Wickham who used the building as his home and surgery. The house was set in three acres of land, had six bedrooms, servants' quarters, stables, tennis and croquet lawns. An ornamental wood covered some of the ground between Holmeswood Road and New Road.

(New Road had been constructed for a proposed visit of Queen Victoria and Prince Albert to the Hesketh family at the New Hall. Alas, the visit was cancelled due to the death of Prince Albert in 1861.)

Dr Wickham was the village doctor between 1881 and 1901. He died tragically on 10 October 1921 aged 72 years and was buried in St Mary's churchyard.

In 1915, the property was purchased by the Rev H.H.Hall and his wife who moved from the old rectory because it was cold and damp.

At the start of World War 2, Mr Hadfield bought the house for £700 and turned it into flats for rent. The building was empty for many years but has now been returned to a dwelling.

From 1841-1861, Charles Dandy was the village doctor and he was succeeded in 1871 by his 37 years old son, Thomas. At the beginning of the 20th century, a Dr Croft was the village doctor and in the 1930's Dr Baird held a surgery three times weekly.

Children sledging in front of *The Hermitage*, with the Hesketh Arms beyond.

Mere Sands Wood

The wood was and is still known locally as *'Yen's wood'* so called after James Caunce whose nick name was *'Yen'*. (Due to the large number of people with the surname, Caunce, most families had a nickname. Some of the names still used today are *'Bacca'*, *'Game'*, *'Stubbs'*, *'Jody'*, *'Pop'*, and *'Pigeon'*). *'Yen'* lived down Sluice Lane and was a gamekeeper on the Hesketh estate. He later lived at the New Hall before moving to live in *'Keepers Cottage'*, now *'Mere Sands Kennels'*. He was known to be an ill tempered man who dealt harshly with local people who were in the wood to poach or even to gather wild blackberries.

James Caunce *('Yen')*, a gamekeeper on the estate, pictured with his dog in the grounds of the New Hall

The field to the right of the present road was known as *'the pheasant field'* because it was where the gamekeepers reared young birds for the game shoots. In 1897 the game bag was 1,485 pheasants, 969 partridge, 635 hares and 108 rabbits. With other game, the total bagged was 3,347.

A map of 1845 shows a pair of cottages at the corner of Spencer's Lane and the wood and on the same corner there was a tree nursery for the estate.

During World War 1 many trees were felled from the centre of the wood and the area was replanted with fir trees.

In the early 1970s planning permission was granted to extract sand from a 10 acre site in the wood over a period of 10 years. Before this time scale lapsed, the wood was sold to Mr Norton and Mr Harris who subsequently formed the *'Rufford Sand Company'*. They wanted to take sand from the whole wood but following discussions with the *'Lancashire Trust for Nature Conservation'*, planning permission was granted in 1977 to excavate only 55 ½ acres. The ownership of the wood, now with lakes, was transferred to the trust in 1982.

No 4 Church Road
This building was originally a pair of semi-detached, thatched cottages. The present building was built in the late 18th century and has a low pitched, *'hipped'* slate roof. (the arris of the roof from ridge to eaves) In the 1920's the cottage on the right had been used as a shop where sweets were sold from the living room. The property was then used by *'Williams Deacons Bank'* on three mornings each week. The name later changed to *'Williams and Glynns Bank'* before finally closing in the1970s. It is now a house.

May Cottage, Church Road
Built in the late 18th century, the cottage was the home and workplace for several generations of the Mayson family, from Richard and his son Henry in 1841 to another Richard in 1901. They were the village boot and shoemakers. The workshop was in the present tower–like building and fittings were done in a room in the house. The two buildings are much the same as when they were built in the late 18th century. Boots and shoes were still made there during and after the Second World War. The property is now a dwelling.

Rufford Mill
The mill was situated along the turnpike road to the south of the main village opposite to the present junction of Liverpool Road and New Road. Constructed of wood in 1720, the first building had sails and the whole building turned round on a wheel. The original millstone was recently found and had the words *'Rufford'* and *'Blundell'* carved on it. Following an

80

examination it was re-buried in the field at Freckleton where it was discovered.

Richard Alty, a miller, was living there on 1 May 1776, Richard Meadow in 1841, James Wignall in 1851 and Edward Hesketh in 1881. By 1901 the corn dealer was Thomas Melling who also ran the grocer's shop at Mill Stores.

A two storey brick building replaced the original one and this second millstone is set into the wall of the smithy. The corn was delivered via an entrance on *'Mill Lane'* (now *'Mill Hey'*) on higher ground and the milled flour was carted away through a lower exit onto Preston Road.

Flour was milled on the site until the end of the 19th century. After the mill closed and the brick building became obsolete, a steam threshing machine was housed on the ground floor and the upper floor was used as a club room. The adjacent semi-detached houses known as *'Lawn Villas'*, were partly built from bricks taken from the mill building when it was demolished.

From the 1920s Walter Southworth ran his haulage business from the old mill site and following the closure of the business, the site became a housing development, *'Whitefield Close'*, in about 1990.

Mill Cottage, Preston Road

Henry Porter's map of 1763 showed the cottage as one of only two properties on the left hand side of the road leading south from the village. Originally built as a mill worker's cottage, it was the home of Robert Bridge and his family at the beginning of the 20th century. It is now known as *'Bower House'*

The Apiary, Folly Lane

Situated at the junction of Folly Lane and Mill Hey, *'The Apiary'* was built in the 1800s as a lodging house to accommodate workers from various parts of the country who had come to the village to work for the Heskeths who were repairing the New Hall and Beech House. The 1881 census showed that six families lived on the site; Thomas Baldwin, an agricultural labourer and his family of three, Robert Bridge, an indoor servant with his family, another Robert Bridge, his wife, son and daughter and William Bridge, farm labourer and his family. Also living there were Margaret Caunce, a grocer and corn merchant, and her two children, five servants and Edward Hesketh, a miller and his family of six.

The property was later used as a *'post and telegraph office'* when Mr Haworth was post master.

In 1946 it became the home and surgery of Tom Hey the local veterinary surgeon and his wife, Elsie. Elsie still lives there.

Joiner's Workshop (Brick Kiln Lane-over the Sluice)

When William Moss retired from his village joinery and wheelwright business in 1931, one of his employees, Billy Martland, opened his own joinery and undertaking business in Brick Kiln Lane. He was followed by Bill Griffin who took over the post office in 1954. The joinery business on the site closed but Bill continued as undertaker while he was at the post office.

Saw Pit

This commercial saw pit, situated on Liverpool Road between the wheelwright's shop and New Road, was established early in the 19th century to process trees cut down on the estate. The pit was dug into the ground and lay parallel to the road. One man stood in the pit holding one handle of the two handled saw and the other man stood at the top of the pit holding the other end. They then worked the saw in vertical movements. Logs from the park and surrounding area were transported by horse and a special trailer, being rolled into the pit from the trailer parked at the side of the road. The saw thought to have been used on this site is in Rufford Old Hall and has been dated 1740. At one time it was used by William Barron (born

1864) a joiner and carpenter of Mill Hill Cottage. The saw pit had closed by the beginning of the 20th century.

Park View, Flash Lane

This house was built as a home for the schoolmasters of Rufford. It is uncertain if Mr Abbott, who was the school master in 1841, lived at the above address, but Mr Haskell who was the teacher in 1891 and 1901, lived there with his family. In the 1920s, Mr Edge, the schoolmaster, and his wife lived down Mere Lane in an ex World War 1 army hut that had been moved from Lathom Park. They later moved to live down Brick Kiln Lane. Mr Brindle also lived at Park View.

The Brick Croft

Now used as an irrigation pit, this is situated to the right off Holmeswood Road. The excavated clay was used to make bricks which were said to be of poor quality.

There was a growth in brick making between the 17th and 18th centuries and bricks were often fired where they were needed in temporary kilns, or *'running clamps'*. Bricks were stacked around a stack of firewood, covered and left to burn. Poor quality bricks were often the result as it was impossible to control the temperature. *'Brick Kiln Yard'* and *'Brick Kiln Hey'* (down the present *'Brick Kiln Lane'*) are identified on a map of 1763.

One account that was recorded on 14 September 1814 in the Brick Account Book of William Shakeshaft, land agent for the Hesketh estate, showed that it had cost £242.9s.0d. to make 236,825 bricks. This amount included the cost of carting clay, preparing the ground, carting soil and cutting sods of earth for the 5 kilns in Rufford Hall Park. In 1839, Richard Bridge was living at the brick croft. These brick kilns were owned by the Hesketh estate. Part of a brick track is all that remains of the

Holmeswood Road site and there is no remaining evidence of the site down Brick Kiln Lane.

Shrub House, Church Road

This property was situated across the road from the *'Spread Eagle Inn'* and was the brew house. The *'maltster'* or *'brewer'* lived in a cottage at the side. In 1906 it was described as *"a large old fashioned double fronted residence built of brick with a slate roof and partly clad with ivy and walled fruit trees"*. The property included stabling for four horses, barn, shippon for five cows, a wash house with copper, a pig cote, a trap house (used to house the horse drawn trap or carriage), flower gardens to front and rear, a croquet lawn and another larger plot of garden at the rear. Although George Hobkirk lived there rent free because he was the land agent for the Hesketh estate, the rental value was £28 per annum. Since the property was sold at the 1906 sale for £500, it has been a private dwelling.

Looking down Church Road with *'Shrub House'*, the old brew house for *'The Spread Eagle Inn'* and *'May Cottage'* on the left

Bay House, Cousins Lane

This small, desirable property had extensive frontage to Cousins Lane. A tithe rent of 13s10d was paid for the six acres site. The family of Mr J Caunce lived there in 1906 and in the 1940s and1950s it was the home of Mr and Mrs George Porter. They had moved from Burscough, where they had a milk round, and they used the Rufford site as a poultry farm. In the

1960s the land was sold. Two roads, Prescot Avenue and Albert Road were made and new houses were built in it.

Ada Caunce of *'Burnley Cottage'* Cousins Lane on the left,chatting to Flo Porter outside a building at her home,*'Bay House,'* Cousins Lane. Is that a home made shovel leaning against the wall?

The Smithy, Liverpool Road

The smithy building , part of which had 3 feet thick walls, was built in 1760 as a small working farm and an inn called the *'Swan Inn'* .When the inn closed in the late 18th century, the property reverted back to a cottage which was leased to James Culshaw, a blacksmith and wheelwright.

He was the great- grandfather of William Moss (1884-1972) who was also a wheelwright, sign writer, undertaker, Methodist preacher and an organist.

In the 1820s, the Hesketh family altered the building to make two separate homes. James Culshaw lived at one side and William Threlfall, his apprentice from Eccleston, lived at the other. The 1851 census showed that a 28 years old journeyman, Henry Lingard, from Treales near Kirkham, was also living there. He had left home to travel to Liverpool on his way to America but had broken his journey at Rufford smithy to seek food and shelter. This was provided on the condition that he worked for his keep. The work was to shoe horses as the resident blacksmith did not have the skills. In 1852 Henry married Hannah, daughter of James Culshaw and never went to America. Besides raising her own family, Hannah also cared for a relative, Seabert Lingard who was born in 1888. When he married in 1910, he lived in a cottage which was on the site of the present day 86 Liverpool Road. Descendents of Henry Lingard have continued to work at the smithy but the business has recently closed.

Mr Lingard shoeing a horse in front of the smithy which was the former *'Swan Inn'*. A young Stanley Lingard is looking on with his sister

Post Offices, Folly Lane and Liverpool Road
The first *'Receiving Office'* (the former name for the post office) in Rufford was established on 28th March 1849.The Rufford office was provided with telegraph facilities in September 1887 and became a Money Office/Savings Bank in January 1891. Towards the end of the 19th century the Rufford office was issued with a single ring hand stamp which was in use until April 1920.

Sarah Abbott, wife of the schoolmaster, was postmistress at the time when the post office was situated at *'The Apiary'*, Folly Lane. The site of the bricked-up post box can still be seen in the front wall of *'Mill House'*, Liverpool Road. The 1881 census identified Robert Abbott as postmaster and by 1892 Thomas Howarth, formerly a tailor, had the job. He lived at *'The Apiary'*. His wife Hannah ran the office in 1901, assisted by her son Robert, the sub- postmaster. Soon after the turn of the century, the post office moved to its present site which had been a 17th century cottage, the home of Mr Southworth, an agricultural labourer.

86

'The Apiary', situated at the junction of HollyLane and Mill Hey.This was the village's first Post and Telegraph Office.

During the 20th century, there have only been four postmasters; Mr Southworth, whose telephonist at one time was Marion Lingard; Mr Cowburn, Mr Griffin and Mr and Mrs Yates who were the last in Rufford. The village has been without a post office since 2nd April 2005.

87

CAFES, SHOPS AND SOME OTHER BUSINESSES

Between the 1920s and 1950s, many Rufford people recognised the opportunity to earn a living from the growing trend in tourism. The position of the country village on the A59 road, mid-way between Preston and Liverpool made it accessible to visitors using either horse drawn wagonettes, cycles and motor cars. Villagers opened shops, cafes, and weekend tearooms. Other enterprising villagers established garages and haulage businesses and provided work and housing for many villagers over many years.

The Maze and Café

In 1934 Mr and Mrs Fred Lee, purchased a piece of land from Mr Wilkinson at the northern end of the village. With William Woodard, the brother of Mrs Lee as manager, they opened a café and shop and created a woodland maze where the path meandered through the trees. There were rabbits, chickens and Muscovy ducks. During World War 2, people from Liverpool would visit and camp in the field behind the café to avoid the bombing. Mr Lee worked with the Polish Displaced Persons Department in Kirkby and during 1948 and 1949 brought people to Rufford where they danced in national costume for the school children. The Lee family lived in

another building further into the wood. After her husband's death, Mrs Lee continued to run the café and maze until the 1960s.

The entrance to the Maze Café and camp.
Young Fred Lee is in the foreground.

88

Red Gables Café, Liverpool Road
In the early 1930s Mrs Worswick, the proprietor of this small café, served teas and light refreshments. She also provided a facility for people to have their photographs taken. The property is now known as *'The Gables'*

Garage and Petrol Station, Liverpool Road
This was started up by the Evermey family and was on the site of the present Ashcroft's haulage yard.

Park Transport Café, Liverpool Road (Now *'Rufford Arms Hotel'*)

'Park View Café and Garage',Liverpool Road, known to villagers and cyclists as *'Nanson's Café'* after the one time owner,Octavious Winder Nanson. Could the two men in flat caps be the mechanics?

Mr Octavius Winder Nanson purchased the land from Lord Hesketh in the 1920s and erected two army huts on the site to facilitate a transport café, a garage repair shop and two petrol pumps. The café was known by all and is still referred to as *'Nanson's Café'*. The large lorry park was often full of lorries in transit from Preston and Liverpool. The café was also used as a meeting place and on Sundays it was full of cyclists from across the county. Mr Nanson presented a trophy, the *'Nanson 100 miles Cup'* to the Liverpool Time Trials Association. Members of the *'Dover Cycling Fellowship'*, including past and present villagers, remember calling on their way home from cycling outings. In a cycling magazine, Park Café was advertised as a café with rooms to let at a cost of 4 shillings and sixpence per night. Mr A Livesey, an apprentice electrician who worked for a Preston firm in 1946 stayed *'bed and breakfast'* whilst working in Rufford, because it took over two hours to travel back to Preston. The cafe was later owned by a Mr Rainford, but trade began to decline following the construction of the M6 motorway which took a lot of traffic off the A59. The café closed in the 1960's. The site was derelict until the *'Rufford Arms Hotel'* opened for business in 1992.

Tea Room, Spark Lane
This was opened by the Hopgood family in the 1940's when they served teas from a room in their home.

Meadow View Café, Liverpool Road
The bungalow is situated opposite Rufford Old Hall and was built in 1938 by Mrs Coxon, aunt of the present owner, Mr Meadley. It was used as a poultry farm and plant nursery before Mrs Coxon opened it as a café in 1945 when her sister moved from Liverpool to help in the business.

Thomas Caunce, Haulage Contractor
Thomas worked for Turners of Bispham before starting his own firm in the mid 1920s. This was originally based in the coach house of the old rectory in Church Road and one of the first drivers was Linton Ashcroft. The family lived in a cottage at the nearby *'Grey Gutter Farm'*. When the business expanded it traded from land in Cousins Lane. The firm ceased trading and the site was derelict for approximately 10 years before a small housing estate, *'Croft Hey,'* was built in 1995.

Rufford Produce, Station Road
Jack Radcliffe purchased the weighbridge from the Hesketh Estate following its sale in 1906. He bought a vehicle and delivered hay, straw and manure. Tom Pickavance was employed to load coal from the goods yard and deliver it to

homes in the area. The company was later run by Jack's nephews, George and Tom. Tom's daughter Sheila and her husband ran the business until their retirement in the 1990s.

Wuthering Heights, Liverpool Road

This news agency and sweet shop opened opposite the village hall in the late 1930s and closed in the early 1960s when the proprietors, the Ashcroft family, moved to live in Lancaster.

Davies' Café, Liverpool Road (between Beech House and the Post Office)

Mr Davies and his wife Lou- Lou had visited Rufford on a cycling outing from Liverpool. After the First World War they returned, purchased the property and ran a shop from the house. Customers waited in the living room, asked for what they wanted and the purchases were then brought from the kitchen. Situated at the side of the cottage, the café was in a wooden cabin and had a veranda at the side. In the garden there was a dove cote and flag pole. Lizzie Coulton rented another cabin in the grounds, which she then leased to the Girl Guides for their Monday evening meetings and to Mrs Hall, wife of the rector, for occasional dances called *'tupenny hops'*. The building was demolished in 1967.

Craig Wen Café, Liverpool Road (next to the Post Office)

The café was situated in a wooden cabin in the garden at the side of the main cottage and was accessed by four steps. John Lingard, a blacksmith, and his wife Mary lived in the cottage and she did the cooking for the café in her kitchen. It was Mary, born in Wales, who suggested the name *'Craig Wen'* as she likened the place to a café on a crag. In 1908 Jack and Mary moved to open a café in Southport and for the next few years the proprietors were M and A Jackson (home address *'Grey Gutter Cottage'*) who also provided accommodation at the rear of the café. Their wooden sign advertised that they provided teas, served customers promptly, catered for large parties, were licensed to sell tobacco but were closed on Sundays. John Lingard also sold and repaired cycles from the site.

Davies' Café, known locally as *'Lou –Lous'*, with Grey Gutter Farm on the right before it was demolished to straighten the road.

Rufford Café where the food was cooked in the house kitchen and taken to customers in the wood cabin on the right. The high handle-bar type of cycle were known as *'sit-up-and-beg'* bikes and a cycle with an attached child seat is obviously not a new invention!! This photo was probably taken not far from 1900.

A later view of the Rufford café, then known as *'Craig Wen'*, when the owners were M.and A. Jackson. A window replaced the front door,which had been moved to the side.

Butcher's shop (at corner of Liverpool Road and Thornton Close)

This property had been a cycle shop before World War 1 and then Mrs Hall ran it as a baby linen shop during the war. In the 1960s it was run by Bert Davies and his son Norman as a butcher's shop and later by Graham Holden as a mini supermarket. The property was demolished and a house was built on the site in the late 1980s.

Central Garage, Liverpool Road

The garage has been in the Sephton family for many years. The 1881 census showed that the Richard Sephton who started the business was born in 1878. Their home was a thatched roofed cottage, later *'tinned over'*, and was situated in front of the present bungalow *'Moor Cottage'*. The old cottage was demolished in 1962 when the bend in the road was straightened. The business opened as a cycle repair shop which sold *'Raleigh'* cycles. Dick Sephton repaired motor vehicles, had petrol pumps and a taxi service. Mrs Sephton ran a chip shop and had a small *'eating'* room. Dick had the first generator in the village for making his own electricity that was also piped across the road to supply *'The Hermitage'* when Mrs Hall was living there. He named the generator *'The Rufford Twin'* to commemorate the birth of his twin daughters, Betty and Bessie. The name was engraved on a brass plaque attached to the generator. The majority of villagers kept pigs in their gardens to supplement their diets and Dick was the local pig killer. As people had no way to preserve the meat, they would share it with family and neighbours who in turn would reciprocate at a later date. The business is now operated by the third generation of the family.

Weighbridge and shop

This was on the site of the present police station opposite the 'Hesketh Arms'. It was on the main road through the village, owned by the Hesketh estate and operated by the inn keeper. When this horse and cart weighbridge closed at the end of the 19th century, the adjacent shed was used as a lockup shop that sold sweets and drinks. It was run by the Ashton family who brought the merchandise daily from their home and other shop in Moss Lane Burscough. In the early twentieth century it was a meeting place for the young men of the village.

Avondale Café and Cyclists' Rest, Liverpool Road (opposite the Hermitage)

The occupants of the property were Elizabeth and her husband Matthew Fearns, who was a saddler and harness maker in 1891. Cycling had become prominent in the 1890s and Betty opened her house as a tea room. A sign outside the house said *'Teas provided'*. Following the death of her husband in 1899, she married into the Lingard family. During the 1930s, the café was known as *'Fearn's Avondale'* and an advert in the 1939 cycling magazine *'Kuklos Annual'* stated that in addition to teas being provided, rooms could be rented for three shillings per night. A special room was available for cycling parties and clubs and for Sunday school parties.

'Avondale Café' with its sign by the telegraph pole and the entrance on Holly Lane on the right.

Mill House Stores, Liverpool Road (opposite the smithy)
The house was built in the early to mid -18th century and in the 1800s, bread that had been made from flour milled at the nearby mill and baked in the brick bread ovens on site was sold in the bakery. In 1925 it was a general and grocery shop run by Henry Southworth. In 1937 the grocer, baker and provision dealer was Ted Wells from Burscough whose advert said *'To keep well, eat Wells!'*. The shop was managed by Mr Hurst who lived in the house. Jack Lingard also worked in the shop and later ran it with his brother Harry. Jack was the sole shop keeper after Harry moved to Parbold. Jack later expanded the business to include home deliveries. Following his retirement he still lived in the house but the shop was used by a picture framing firm. The building was demolished, the site was added to the surrounding land and Whitefield Close was built in 1990.

Mr and Mrs Lingard with a baby sitting on the wall in front of the smithy about 1940.
In the background the out buildings at *'Mill House Stores'* and the former First World War *'fire station'* on the end.

J Baker and Son, Cycles and Motor Accessories, Liverpool Road
This garage was situated on Liverpool Road between *'Lawn Villas'* and the entrance to the old mill. James Baker started the business by repairing cycles and serving petrol from the one pump. After his son *'Jimmy'* finished his apprenticeship at Ascroft's garage in Holmes, Tarleton, the firm started to repair

motor cars on the premises. In 1939, Jimmy purchased land on Causeway Lane from Bill Moon and built *'Causeway Garage'*. In 1941, Joe Grisedale was employed as an apprentice mechanic and purchased the business in 1966. The local newspaper published an article in November 1981 highlighting Joe's restoration of a 1937 Guy motor lorry named *'Old Sal'*. The business was sold in 1985.

Walter Southworth, Haulage Contractor, Liverpool Road
In 1910 Walter started his business by transporting agricultural produce grown on the family's land to Preston market using a horse and cart. He bought a *'Leyland'* motor lorry in 1918 and went into partnership with another Rufford man, Charlie Rimmer. They started the haulage and threshing machine business in a garage on Mill Hey Lane and purchased part of the old mill site on the A59. When the partnership was dissolved, Charlie carried on trading from Mill Hey and Walter moved to the old mill site. In 1932 a new family home, *'Park House'*, was built on the opposite side of the A59. This later became the registered office; the firm closed in 1989.

Walter Southworth's Leyland lorry and trailer transporting a load of Guinness to Blackpool in the 1930's.

97

Tom Parker with a load of bran on a Leyland lorry belonging to Charlie Rimmer whose yard was down Mill Hey. The lorry had previously belonged to Dickenson's of Bolton.

Martland's Transport, Liverpool Road.

William Martland started the haulage business in the 1930s from a site near Dam Brook Bridge on the A59. He later went into partnership and the firm became *'Martland and Foster'*. The land was then sold and, in 1990, part of the site became *'Whitefield Close'*.

London Coffee House, Liverpool Road

Mr and Mrs Cairns opened the café that was situated on the site of the old Causeway Wharf, known locally as the *'muck hey'*. The wharf was between the canal and the road leading to Burscough. The coffee house closed during World War 2 when Mr Cairns, who was German by birth, was interned, probably on the Isle of Man.

Transport Café, Liverpool Road

Betty Coulton ran a transport café in a wooden building that was situated next to the *'Empress Café'*. The wooden building had been moved from the site of the *'London Coffee House'* after Mr Cairns had been interned during the Second World War

Empress Café / Tango / Oasis, Liverpool Road

James Stock built the café in 1922 and named it *'The Empress Café'*. It consisted of three large wooden buildings; one was used as a boiler house, the one to the front was used as a sweet shop and café and the one at the rear was used as a second café. It was later sold it to Mr and Mrs Leadbetter who, having transformed and extended it, renamed it the *'Tango Café'* and catered for lunches and suppers. There was a dance floor with cubicles, settees and curtains at one side and a resident dance band. frequented by people from all over West Lancashire. In the 1950s several boxers, including Billy Elloway from Litherland, used the building for *'sparring'*. The property was owned by Forshaws from Burscough in the early 1960s.

They installed two petrol pumps, used the building as a supermarket and renamed it *'The Oasis'*. The site now consists of a new road called *'Oasis Close'* and a row of cottages built in 1987.

Grocery and Sweet Shop, Brick Kiln Lane

In the 1930s, *'Edie'* Bridge moved from her previous home in Church Road to a new address in Brick Kiln Lane, near the junction with Holmeswood Road. Until the early 1960s she used a room in her home as a shop selling groceries and sweets.

Sweet Shop, Brick Kiln Lane

In the early twentieth century, sweets were sold from the living room of a cottage situated opposite the Methodist Chapel on Brick Kiln Lane.

McLeod's Shop, Cousins Lane

William *'Billy'* McLeod worked for Mr Southworth at *'Mill House Stores'* before he and his family moved from there in the 1930s to open their own grocery shop at their home in Cousins Lane near to the junction of Tootle Lane. Billy could often be seen in his blue van making home deliveries. Following his death, his wife continued to run the shop until the 1960s. She died in 1973. The property then reverted back to a house and was used as a milk depot. At the present day it is again a private dwelling.

Workshop and garage of James Baker. His son, also James, is pictured leaning against the petrol pump. It was situated between the old mill and *'Lawn Villas'* on Liverpool Road.

LEISURE AND PLEASURE ORGANISATIONS

During the late 19th and early 20th centuries the increase in leisure time led to an increase in the number of local groups and societies, amongst them were;-

Rufford Temperance Band
The band was established in the mid 1800s and played at many village events including *'walking days'* and concerts and always at the annual Agricultural Show. They were always ready to co-operate in village and church functions. One New Year's Day they marched around the village to collect donations for new uniforms which consisted of navy tunics with red epaulettes and a navy peaked cap with metal badge. In 1911 the conductor was James Southworth though by 1919, Tom Salthouse, who lived in a converted railway carriage sited at the rear of *'Thornton Farm'*, had taken over the position. Practices were held at the Hesketh Arms, but when this facility was no longer available in the early 1950s, the group, then conducted by Harry Draper from Moss Lane, disbanded.

Rufford Temperance Band, who play ed at all the village functions and on *'walking days'*

Tennis Club, Liverpool Road
In 1939 the *'Girls Friendly Society'* (GFS) decided to rent a field to make into a tennis court but decided to postpone making a hard court until the tennis club was established. William

Moss, the wheelwright, rented some ground at the rear of his property in Liverpool Road to make into two grass courts, other men in the village gave sods for the surface and Mr E Moss gave nets and posts to the club. The members started playing in July 1939. Initially it was a females only club but when membership numbers fell, men were invited to join. At the beginning of the 1940s, the grass courts were replaced with two hard courts that were laid on Parish Council land opposite the recreation ground. Village interest in tennis waned after a few years, the hard court surfaces collapsed and were never repaired.

The tennis club in the back garden of the Wheelwrights' home on Liverpool Road. It was made for the use of the *Girls Friendly Society*

Village children dressed in their Sunday best for a walking day procession. The rear of the school in the background

Dancing/Drama Classes

Mrs Hall, the wife of the rector had been an actress before her marriage and during the 1920s and 1930s she organised dancing classes and plays which were held in the school. When she left the village in the mid -1930s, a *'Madam Goodall'* taught all types of dancing in a wooded hut at the rear of *'The Grove'* Holmeswood Road.

Rufford Agricultural Show

The show first started in 1846 after the demise of the previously held *'Mediaeval Fair'* and was held annually except during the years of the 1st and 2nd World Wars. In 1901 it was reported in the *'Ormskirk Advertiser'* as the *'Rufford Fair and Cattle Show'* in connection with the *'Rufford and District Agricultural Society'* and was held in the road and on a small field adjoining the Hesketh Arms. The president that year was Rev Hogg-Goggin. In the horned cattle section, Thomas Yates came second with his two year old bull; in the horse section, Philip Ascroft came third with the cleanest horse and cart and in the butter section, Alice Ascroft came second with her three pound basket of butter. The thirty seventh show in 1911, held in the centre of the park, was attended by Thomas Fermor Hesketh JP whose father had been largely instrumental in forming the society. There was thunder around on the day of the show and it was reported that' *Heavenly Artillery'* could be heard. During speeches at the lunch at the Hesketh Arms, the society congratulated themselves on their *'sound financial position'*. The silver cup for the champion filly was won by T.C. Porter of Rufford, Mrs Ascroft of Holly Farm came first with her two years old bull and Henry Balmer came third with his six white eggs. All records were broken when the 42nd show took place on 7th June 1919 and gate receipts totalled £150. It was held on a new site as Major Fermor Hesketh had broken up the previous piece of ground for food production. He promised to provide a permanent site for the following

103

year. The chairman was T C Porter, the secretary was Henry Caunce of *'Bay Tree Farm'* and the treasurer was John Radcliffe. The lunch was again held at the Hesketh Arms where the committee and guests were served by the landlords Mr and Mrs Radcliffe. There were classes for horses, cattle, sheep, pigs, poultry, rabbits, bread, butter, hams and eggs and, in the evening, show jumping took place in the parade ring. Villagers were recruited to act as *'messengers'* for the show and in 1945 when the late Fred Lee was a messenger, his job was to collect rabbits from the station and take them to the showground.

Other than the war years, the show continued until 1956.

Rufford Girls Brigade. May 1935-Back-?, Elsie Ashcroft, Kitty Yates,?,?, Margaret Bridge. Middle-?, Marion Pickavance, Beatie Pickavant, ?,?, Front-? Ashcroft,?, Margaret Caunce

Rufford Medieval Fair and Market

As a fundraising exercise, Rufford Village Hall committee decided to organise a day-long medieval style fair and market. It took place on the park on the first Monday in May 1976. The attractions included craft and antique marquees, medieval music, side shows, stalls, dog and goat shows, horse displays in the arena, and exhibitions by Preston and Leyland Morris

104

men. The shows were held annually, with the exception of 1977 the Queen's silver jubilee year, and attracted between 10.000 and 14.000 people to the village. The new hall park was used for parking the thousands of vehicles that entered the village. The last show was held in 1989 as the parking facility would not be available in future years.

Fire Brigade

During the First World War, the '*fire station*' was a large box-like structure that was fixed to the brick wall of the grocery store which was adjacent to '*Mill House*'. There was an opening on the front with a small glass window that could be broken in emergency. Inside there was a hose that could be attached to a tap after piped water had reached the village in 1905. There had been a serious fire risk to the many older, thatched roofed properties.

A wooden cabin in the park was the headquarters of the Fire Brigade during the Second World War. Local men manned the station each night from 6pm to 6am and when needed, the mobile pumps were either pushed manually or towed behind a vehicle. The men went to Ormskirk for weekly drill practice and on one occasion when the pump got stuck in mud on the park, they unhooked it and left it behind.

Jubilee Jazz Band

The band was created to celebrate the silver jubilee of King George and Queen Mary in 1935 but they only played on that one day. The band marched round Rufford where spectators were six deep along the footpaths. People came from other villages that did not have events of their own. Although it was mainly girls who dressed in a red, white and blue uniform, three men did assist with some instruments. They were Tommy Walsh the leader, Sidney Sephton the drummer and Jack Almond the kettle drum player.

Rufford Ladies Jazz Band 1935; Back- Mary Yates, Mary Caunce, Margery Bourn, Beatrice Pickavant, Kitty Yates, Margaret Bridge, Ellen Coulton, Elsie Gatley, Dorothy McLeod, Jane Mason, Annie Parsons, Margaret Martland, Lily Bridge, Ellen Martland, Florence Singleton, Edith Bridge, Elizabet Hesketh, Irene Hull, Alice Caunce, Margaret Stazicker, Mary Sephton,. Front- Elsie Ashcroft, Nellie Ashton, Florence Mawdsley, Sidney Sephton (drummer), Thomas Walsh (conductor), Marion Pickavance, Jenny Moss, Jack Almond (kettle drum), Alice Moss, Jessie Johnson (trainer)

Morris Dancers

Mr and Mrs Smith started a girls troupe of Morris dancers in the 1930s. They danced at garden parties and marched on village walking days. They were members of the '*Northern Regional Carnival Association*' and danced as far away as the Isle of Man. For many years they were trained by Matt Holmes, assisted by Henry Caunce. The troupe disbanded in 1997.

Rufford Morris dancers in
the late 1930s

106

Football Club

The club began playing in 1915 and the three teams, juniors, seniors and a school team played on one pitch in the park. Interest waned, but in 1937 the club was reformed and played friendly matches that season to prepare for full league games the following year. The team, playing in a blue and white strip, had a good 1947-1948 season when they reached the final of the *'Guildhall'* cup in the Preston and District League. They were supported by Norman Chadwick, team mascot, plus eight coach loads of villagers. The final, played at Preston North End's ground, was won by Farington. Although the club lost again in the 1971-72 cup final, they won the Guildhall cup in the 1972-73 season.

Rufford football team who were finalists in the *'Guildhall Cup' in* 1947-48 season.

Back- Les Sewel, Harry Hargraves. John Iddon, Lynton Ashcroft, Walter Aspinall, Trevor Bridge. Front- Albert Ashcroft, Billy Caunce, Joe Martland, Bob Disley, Joe Pickavance, and Norman Chadwick the mascot

An early (1930s?) Rufford football team, alas with unnamed players

Parish Council

On Tuesday 4th December 1894 the electors of Rufford met at the boys' school to nominate people for the proposed parish council. The first meeting was held on 19th December. James Caunce was elected vice chairman, John Morrison (manager of the *'Liverpool and District Bank'*), treasurer, Thomas Hobkirk, clerk, plus Hugh Prescot and Henry Caunce. Richard Yates was elected as chairman of the parish council and also as the village representative on the *'Ormskirk Urban District Council'*. For the first 20-30 years, the minutes of the meetings were very brief and often had two main topics; - the money to be paid for catching rats/moles and finances. The accounts for 1895 showed that income was £56 and expenditure was £53. In the early years, the parish council elected a *'May'* warden, his role is unknown, and two parish *'overseers'* whose role was to use public funds to assist the poor of the village. In 1899, the Ormskirk Urban District Council contacted the parish council for a contribution of £3/6/5d for the upkeep of the steam fire engine. (Ormskirk was established in 1861 and, following a restructure of local authorities in 1974, the name changed to *'West Lancashire District Council'*). Meetings continued throughout the First World War and in 1916, an Army Recruiting Officer wanted to attend a meeting to be introduced to all able bodied young men of the village. The outcome is unknown and no further action was taken, so perhaps his request was declined. Still obsessed with vermin, the council accounts showed that in 1918, one penny per dozen was paid for rats (with no tails) or sparrows, three pence per dozen for sparrow heads, two pence per dozen for young sparrows and one penny per dozen for sparrow eggs! Following the formation of the council, meetings were only held periodically and then three monthly. During the 1950s, ten meetings were held each year with no meetings during July and August as the majority of members were farmers busy with the harvest. There are now twelve monthly meetings. It was only in the late 1980s that the public were allowed into meetings although they were not allowed to speak except through a councillor. By 1994, time was made in the meeting to enable members of the public to ask questions.

Men's Social Club

Following lengthy discussions between Rev Proctor and the men of the village, the club finally opened on Saturday 10th October 1908. The venue for this non-political, non-denominational gathering was the upper floor of the old brick built mill building on Mill Hey. The ethos of the club was to encourage young men to spend their evenings in '*wholesome*' amusement instead of loitering in the dark and was open every night except Sunday.

When Walter Southworth purchased the building in the early 1930s, the room on the upper floor was no longer available to be used for the club. In 1939, Mr Moss, the wheelwright who lived next door to the smithy, provided accommodation for a new meeting room situated in a building between '*Park House*' and the smithy. A snooker table was provided for members and women were allowed in for sewing classes and to play whist and dominoes. During the Second World War, the building was used by the A.R.P. (Air Raid Precautions) group.

Rufford Working Men's Club

Following a disagreement and perhaps to annoy Walter Southworth, Robert Pickavance of '*Roseacre Farm*', Sluice Lane, leased a plot of land at the corner of Sluice Lane and New Road to the trustees of the newly formed '*Rufford Men's Social Club*'. The wooden building had one room with two snooker tables and another room where members played cards. The teams played in the '*Asland Snooker and Billiard League*'. The club was open to young men of 17 years and over on three evenings during the week. The building was dismantled and moved to Hesketh Bank when the club closed in the mid 1960s.

Cricket Club

Rufford Park was the venue for the cricket club when it was established on 2nd June 1883 and it has been a member of the *'Southport and District Cricket League'* from the onset. The two-roomed wooded pavilion provided changing facilities for both the home and away teams. Villagers also remember games being played in the New Hall grounds near to *'Rufford Lodge'* and on ground belonging to *'Brick Kiln Farm'*. The club experienced problems playing on the park when the Agricultural Show was in existence. One year, the Society dug a water jump in the middle of the cricket area and then when someone hired a steam roller to flatten the square, its rollers left large indentations in the grass. Following the re-grouping after the war, the club was known as *'Rufford Sports Club'*; encompassing cricket, football and tennis. Thomas and James Prescott provided a pasture in Tootle Lane as a short term solution, but the League were not happy with a tent as a changing room. The club returned to play in the park but Rufford Parish Council refused permission for matches to be played on Sundays. Thomas Caunce then made land available on Cousins Lane and the pavilion was moved to the present cricket field in 1952. The club is still flourishing and has five teams; first and second XI's, under 18's, under 15's and under 13's.

The Oddfellows

The *'Travellers Rest Lodge'* of the *'Order of Oddfellows'* was a long-established club for the young men of the village. In June 1858, they held a Lodge anniversary celebration meeting at the Hesketh Arms and then marched to the Old Hall and to Burscough Bridge before returning to Rufford for dinner cooked by the landlady, Mrs Barron. Dinner was followed by

110

singing to the music of Eccleston band and the 160 present disbanded in the early hours of the following morning. By 1909 the meetings moved to the school to reduce costs and to encourage new members. James Baldwin, secretary, made himself available to the young men to explain the benefits of joining. By 1937 the group came under the auspices of '*The Manchester Unity of Oddfellows Friendly Society*' and offered a range of insurances to its members who still held their meetings in the school at Rufford.

Women's Institute
Although the Lancashire Federation was formed in 1920, it was not until 1953 that the Rufford branch was established. Mrs Margerison was the first president and membership was by nomination from other members. All the ladies wore hats and were referred to as '*Mrs*'. Today no nomination is required. Due to lack of space, the 55 members have moved from their original meeting place in the '*Scout hut*' in Flash Lane to the village hall. Meetings are held monthly.

Nudist Camp
Although not a village organisation, this facility has been in existence in Rufford since the 1930s. The club is advertised as being set in ten acres of woodland, is open all year and has a solar-heated swimming pool. It is now owned by the '*Lancashire Sun Society*', who have groups throughout the county.

During subsequent decades, other groups, clubs and organisations have been established in the village. Some of those that are no longer active include the football team, the pigeon club, Guides, a weekly teenage disco, a youth club, The Girls' Brigade, dancing classes, evening classes, drama group, the Second World War organisations included the Home Guard, Rufford War Comforts Committee, the Rufford branch of the British Legion and the Rufford Red Cross Working Party. Other organisations that are still active include the Scout Groups, Brownies, Rainbows, Good Companions, Pre-school Play Group, Mothers and Toddlers, Line Dancing and Pensioners' Luncheon Club.

Although the character of the village is changing, echoes of the old independence and community spirit are still heard and will no doubt continue through the efforts of the village clubs, council and projects.